Raising Black Girls

By Dr. Jawanza Kunjufu

IMAGES
Chicago, Illinois

T0159409

ISBN #: 1-934155-74-8

ISBN #: 978-1934-155-745

Contents

Introduction

Introduction

I have written more than 37 books, and one-third of them have been geared toward the growth and development of African American males. As a father of two sons and a grandfather of a grandson, I have had a personal interest in this important subject.

Over my 40-year career I've been asked hundreds of times why I haven't written a book about African American females. I have asked my staff at African American Images to write about Black females and they have written several books; but I was led to write my first book on the subject, *Educating Black Girls*, in the summer of 2014. And it became a national best seller. The book was written for educators, psychologists, social workers, and all those concerned about the academic development of African American females.

While researching *Educating Black Girls*, I realized that there was too much information for just one book. Thus, I decided to write a second book for parents, grandparents, caregivers, foster parents, and all those who are involved in parenting African American females. In 2007, I wrote *Raising Black Boys*, so perhaps it was destiny that I would eventually write *Raising Black Girls*, the book you are now reading. While it is written primarily for adults, I encourage you to share information that you think would be appropriate with your daughter, granddaughter, or niece.

I was moved to write *Educating Black Girls* and Raising Black Girls because all is not well with African American females. While the media has emphasized the acute problems facing African American males, those facing Black females have gone virtually unnoticed. Too many of our girls are having problems with reading and math, retention, special education placement, suspension, expulsion, dropping out, teen pregnancy, STDs, fighting, gang involvement, obesity, relationships, and incarceration. For these reasons and many more, I felt a need to research and explore and try my best to fully understand the lives of African American females. This book reflects my concern and compassion for their development, empowerment, and overall well-being.

To understand Black girls, we must first examine not only who is raising them, but *how* they are being raised. There are four types of parenting styles: authoritative, authoritarian, permissive, and neglectful.

Authoritative parenting is demanding, responsive, and child-centered. Authoritative parents have high expectations of maturity and excellence. They can empathize with their children's feelings, but they do not allow tantrums and unacceptable behavior. They teach their children how to regulate feelings and find appropriate outlets to solve problems. Authoritative parents encourage children to be independent, but still place controls and limits on their actions. They set clear standards for their children, monitor the limits they set, and also allow children to develop autonomy. Children are expected to be mature, independent, and act in age-appropriate ways. Punishments for misbehavior are measured and consistent, not arbitrary or violent. When punishing a child, these parents explain their motives for the punishment.

Authoritarian parenting, also called strict parenting, is characterized by high expectations of conformity and compliance to parental rules and directions while allowing little open dialogue between parent and child. Authoritarian parenting is a restrictive, punitive parenting style in which obedience to rules is the primary goal. Corporate punishment, yelling, scolding, and even cursing are common.

Permissive parents are not very demanding, but they are nurturing and accepting and responsive to the child's needs and wishes. Permissive parents do not require children to regulate themselves or behave appropriately, often resulting in "spoiled brat" behaviors. Children of permissive parents tend to be more impulsive, and as adolescents, there may be misconduct and drug use. Children never learn to control their own behavior, and they always expect to get their way.

Neglectful parents are uninvolved, detached, dismissive, hands off, disengaged, undemanding, unresponsive, low in warmth, and they do not set limits. Their attention always seems to be elsewhere. Neglectful parents often dismiss their children's emotions and opinions. Parents are emotionally unsupportive of their children and only provide for their basic needs.

Now honestly ask yourself, "Which parenting style best represents how I've been raising my daughter?"

Some parents have one style with one child and another style with another child. They had one style in their '20s, another in their '30s, and yet another in their '40s. They had one style when they were employed and another when unemployed. They had one style when they were happily married, another when a divorced single parent, and then another when they remarried or when a grandparent pitched in.

Now explain to your daughter the four parenting styles, then ask her, "Which type of parent do you think I am?"

I also would like for you to give a copy of this book to every permissive, neglectful and authoritarian parent you know.

Chapter 1: Black Girls Speak

This is my most enjoyable chapter. For the past 12 to 18 months, I've been traveling around the country just listening to Black girls. I truly enjoy talking to them, listening to them, appreciating them, respecting them, and being mesmerized by them. There is so much joy and beauty in Black females.

In this chapter, I'd like to share their thoughts in their own words.

My mother is my best friend.

My mama is a trip.

- My dad is so cool.

- I want to be a doctor, married, with two children.

I want to grow up to be somebody.

I like First Lady Michelle Obama. She's pretty and smart.

- I want to be accepted, but I don't want to compromise.

- I want to travel and get out of this neighborhood.

- I like him because he's real, and he respects me.

- She's my home girl because she has my back.

- I like wearing my mama's clothes and jewelry.

- I'm glad my parents stayed together.

Don't get mad because I'm lighter than you.

Boys will try to destroy your reputation.

If you are light skinned with good hair and a pointed nose, be ready to fight.

I became a fighter to stop boys from touching me.

I am not a b**, beotch, or beeyatch.

I want adult privileges. I'm grown. I'm 14 years old.

- We come from two different generations with different issues.

- We don't know how to love ourselves because nobody's loving us.

- My mother told me my hair was too kinky to wear to church.

- It's hard finding jeans that give me booty room.

- I should be able to wear what I want.

- Do Black guys ever like dark girls?

You can't trust Black girls talking to your man.

I'm running for my life when it starts raining.

I refuse to let my hair go back.

Are guys deaf or stupid?

I said, *No!*

Guys will say anything to get some booty.

I don't like my mama's boyfriend spending the night and eating up all our food.

- I miss my daddy.

- I laugh when I hear a White girl call her mom a b**, knowing I better not try that with my mama.

- I never knew my daddy.

- Everything good in me died in junior high school when I was raped.

- I can't wait to be grown to get out of this house.

- All men are dogs.

- He took my virginity, and he hurt me.

The room smells like bacon when I do my hair with a flat iron.

A baby will change your life forever.

Don't call me out of my name.

I will never let a man hurt me. I will never trust a man.

I will never fight over a man.

Doing my hair takes forever.

My butt is the largest part of my body, and the darkest.

- I would play sports, but I don't want some chick trying to roll up on me in the locker room. I don't play that.

- I like my man to be tough. I don't want no punk.

- I get tired of being called bald headed because I have short hair.

- Black girls always keep some mess going.

- I'm tired of my relaxer burn.

- I get compliments on a weave that I'm not wearing.

- I hate all the rules about my mobile device. If it's mine, I should be able to do what I want with it.

- My mama thinks I'm her maid and babysitter.

- I hate wearing this school uniform.

- I need to lose some weight.

- I need to go to church because I've been cursing all week.

- My mama thinks she knows everything.

- I'm too nerdy for Black kids and too Black for White kids.

- I hate it when my mama hollers at me.

- I used to be thick. Now I'm just fat.

- I wish I knew my daddy.

- I wish my daddy would call me, especially on my birthday.

I'd like for you to review the above comments. Meditate on them, and ask yourself if your daughter feels this way. When was the last time you had an open, honest conversation with your daughter? When is the last time you did more listening and had your daughter do more talking?

I believe Black girls have a message to tell us. They told me that what they need most is someone who will sincerely listen to them and not be judgmental. Unfortunately, if parents are not going to listen to their daughters, then they will share their pearls of wisdom with their peer group.

In the next chapter, we will provide the framework for this book.

Chapter 2: Framework

In this chapter, we will provide the framework and concepts upon which the overall book is based. To begin, the following are just a few thought provoking ideas that will be developed throughout the book.

- She's pretty to be so black.

- I'm so glad she did not come out dark.

- Mama taught me how to make it *without* him, but not how to make it *with* him.

- Why is it so hard for some girls to talk to their mothers?

- Historically, girls would just kill you with their mouths, but now it's with their fists.

- Many girls have an 18-year-old body, 25 years of exposure to television, and a 12-year-old intellect.

- Girls mature and grow up so fast due to poverty, media, father-lessness, and a bad diet.

- It takes a village—not a TV, mobile device, or video game—to raise a child.

- Love is something you do, not say.

- Do not let racism, sexism, colorism, classism, or Black self-hatred define you.

- Children should result from a loving marriage and not casual, unprotected sex.

- When girls grow up without a father present, we have a problem. But when they grow up without God, we have a crisis.

- Don't go to jail holding your man's drugs.

- Some mistakes you can't afford to make once.

- Too sexy, too soon.

- Eighteen is the new 14, and 14 is the new 10.

- Too many uncles and boyfriends are living in Black girls' homes.

- Girls learn to hate or love men from their mothers.

- You are more than the sum of your parts.

- Beauty or brains or both?

- Some females want a man more than God.

- Two females in the house can be combustible.

- What and who motivates Black girls?

- It's hard raising a godly daughter in an ungodly world.

- I will learn to love me before I will look for someone else to love me.

- My mama told me to get a good education and a good job, not to be dependent on a man.

- Why do some Black girls clap when they hear there are more Black men in prison than Black females?

- Bullies and b**s are sad, mean people.

- Girls grow up dreaming of ways to catch a man. Boys grow up dreaming of ways to buy a car.

- Being single is not a disease.

- It's better to develop girls than to repair broken women.

- Why are so many Black females angry at each other?

- Why are so many Black females mad at Black men?

- Evictions are to Black women what incarceration is to Black men. Once evicted it's very difficult to rent again.

- Girls can be tender, soft, sweet, catty, manipulative, rebellious, brutal, and sneaky, all within the same minute.

- Based on dress and physique, I can't tell the female students from the female teachers.

- All girls should learn martial arts and chess.

- Unplug your daughter from a plugged-in world.

- Some girls distance themselves from parents when, in adolescence, they need them the most.
- Obesity is worse than death.

- Most girls spend their entire lives looking for the love they missed from their father.

- What psychological scars do girls have due to fatherlessness?

- Does fatherlessness lead to promiscuity?

- How do mothers overcompensate for fatherlessness?

- What is the impact of allowing a boyfriend to spend the night or live in your home?

- What types of literature are our girls reading?

- Who is determining the dress code for our girls?

- What do our girls believe spiritually?

- Do our girls understand and recognize racism, sexism, classism, and colorism? Do they know how to resist them?

- Girls are unique. They like pretty things, want to be valued, are maternal, and they value relationships.

- Are you a ghetto girl or a good girl?

- The key to failure is trying to please everyone.

- Girls lose their childhood when they have to raise their siblings.

- Teen pregnancy is a generational curse.

- Is abortion being used as birth control?

- When does a girl become a woman? You were born female. You become a girl and mature into a woman.

- You can be 40 years of age and still be a girl.

- Not every girl becomes a woman.

- Shirley Chisholm said sexism begins when the hospital staff announces, "It's a girl!"

- Her appearance will always be the first thing judged, and her body becomes her bargaining chip.

- Some girls have never been outside their neighborhoods.

- Steve Harvey said to wait at least 90 days before having sex. Jesus said to wait until you're married.

- Parenting is the only profession that does not require study and passing an exam to secure a license.

- Every girl needs a female role model.

- Your worth is more than your body.

- Some mothers wear their daughters' clothes, listen to her music, and share the same boyfriend.

- There are two types of females: one who can't live without a man and will do anything for him, and one who prefers a man, but can live without him and will not compromise.

- How can you give your child a better life if you don't have one?

- Her sexuality began when she was drugged at a party.

- Have you no shame? Girl, hold your head up!

- All sexual relationships are based on transactions and negotiations.

- Your thoughts create your future.

- Some mothers teach their daughters to be independent of Black men, but accept racism, sexism, classism, and colorism.

- Many Black men want their females to have nice hips, a big butt, light skin, long, straight hair, and a pointed nose.

- Black hair grows out, not down.

- Girls grow up so fast. One day she was in a car seat. Now she's asking for the car keys.

- To children between 13 and 18 years old, parents are the dumbest, meanest people. After age 30, parents are the smartest, kindest people.

- Eighteen seconds of sex could produce 18 years of child rearing.

From infancy to 21 years, you are your child's parent. After 21 years, you also become her friend.

Take care of you. Don't live your life for and through your children.

Think twice: once for you, then for your child.

One diet shy of the perfect body.

Child rearing days are long, but the years go fast.

Do you want a good kid or good grades?

We want every Black girl to be *at promise*, not *at risk*.

- Sex trafficking has become a $64 billion industry. Men know they can sell drugs only once, but they can sell a woman forever.

- Pregnancy is the number one concern of Black females.

- People's values are reflected in the lyrics of their favorite songs.

Last and perhaps most important, we need to teach Black girls 28, 30, 2, 4:

- **28:** Black females should not get married until they feel good about themselves. That psychological state may not be achieved until they are 28 years old.

- **30:** They should not have children until they're married and have discussed child rearing with their mate. That may occur when they reach 30 years.

- **2:** Only bring into the world the number of children you can manage. Many successful people have decided that number is 2.

- **4:** Babies should not come every nine months. Not only does a woman's body need rest, but babies need plenty of lap time and nurturance for their health, cognitive development, and emotional well-being. Have babies four years apart and they will each receive the nurturing they need. Bonus: they will never be in college at the same time!

Unfortunately too many of our girls have learned 0, 13, 9, 1:

- **0:** It seems like hardly any young African American women are getting married.

- **13:** First pregnancies occur at 13 years of age if not younger.

- **9:** Some young females have as many as 9 babies.

- **1:** They're having 1 baby per year.

The Stanford University marshmallow study documents the importance of teaching children the importance of delayed gratification. Give your children two options. A small reward immediately or a larger reward later. Those children who waited performed better on test scores and achieved higher career goals.

The above concepts will be developed in the following chapters. In the next chapter, we will look at the trends affecting Black girls.

Chapter 3: Trends

Typically trends, statistics, and facts about Black females are skewed in a negative direction. I want to begin this chapter with some positive trends affecting Black women. The following are some exciting and positive changes taking place in Black America, particularly among Black females.

- 2.3 million Black females are in college.
- Spelman and Bennett continue to do a fantastic job as the only two African American women's colleges in the U.S.
- 46 percent of Black college females graduate from college.
- Black females are 66 percent of all African Americans who earn an associate, bachelor's or a graduate degree.
- 1.1 million Black females are entrepreneurs, and they are the fastest growing segment.
- Black females are 31 percent of female military personnel.
- Black females are dominating the WNBA, tennis, and track and field.
- Black females are CEOs of several Fortune 500 companies.
- More than 90 percent of Black mothers stay with their children.
- More than 4,300 Black female officials have been elected to serve at the local, state, and national levels.
- There is a 51 percent decline in Black female teen pregnancy.
- Black females continue to live longer than Black men with a life expectancy of 78 years.

Although we're seeing many positive trends, unfortunately all is not well with Black girls and women in America.

- 1 of every 4 girls in America has an STD; 48 percent of Black female teens has had an STD.
- 1 of every 19 Black females will be incarcerated; 1 in every 45 Hispanic females will be incarcerated; 1 in 111 White females will be incarcerated.

Raising Black Girls

- 50 percent of Black females are pregnant by age 20.
- The leading cause of death among Black babies is abortion and 1,786 children are killed daily.
- 52 percent of all Black pregnancies are aborted.
- 1 of 3 teen mothers graduate from high school, and 80 percent live on welfare.
- In 90 percent of domestic violence cases, the female is the victim.
- In 2013, 854 Black females were victims of homicide. 94 percent knew the assailant.
- Black females have a greater chance of being murdered than all other women and White and Asian men.
- 41 percent of Black females are overweight.
- 100,000 females are in gangs, and 35,000 are Black females.
- 70 percent of Black women can't swim, and this is a safety hazard.
- 47 percent of rape is date rape.
- 16 percent of Black females have an eating disorder.
- 40 percent of all teens consider running away; 2.8 million do annually.
- Sex trafficking is now a $64 billion industry.
- 50 percent of Black teens report the presence of alcohol at parties.
- 20 percent of Black females have used marijuana.
- More than 25 percent of Black females have shoplifted.
- If a woman is HIV positive, 64 percent of the time she's a Black female.
- 61 percent of Black females report a physical altercation with their boyfriend.
- 43 percent of Black females score in the aggressive category on psychological tests.
- The median net worth for single Black females is $5.
- 67 percent of Black females report being sad, depressed or hopeless for two weeks or more.
- One million women of all races are under the prison system; 200,000 are incarcerated and 60,000 are Black females.[1]

Chapter 4: Demographics

Black people, and specifically Black girls, live in a variety of social environments. The Black family is not monolithic.

Income

One-third of African Americans live below the poverty line. Forty-two percent make up the working class.

Some people still do not believe that *The Cosby Show*, which featured wealthy professionals Clair and Cliff Huxtable, showcased a true slice of African American life. Twenty-five percent of African Americans earn more than $75,000 per year.[2] One-fourth of Black girls live in middle- and upper-income households. Unfortunately, one-third live below the poverty line, and 42 percent are in the middle. So as we discuss how best to raise Black girls, it is important to understand that a myriad of experiences are shaping their lives. Income is one of those factors.

Parenting Configurations

Another factor is the parenting dynamic. Following are some parenting configurations that are impacting Black girls today:
- 2 biological parents
- 1 biological parent, 1 stepparent
- Mother and boyfriend
- Father and girlfriend
- Mother and grandparent
- Father and grandparent
- Single mother
- Single father
- Grandparent
- Grandparents
- Other relatives
- Foster parents
- Black adoptive parents
- Non-African American adoptive parents

Raising Black Girls

- Institutionalized parenting
- 2 females
- 2 males

Clearly not all of our girls are being raised by a mother and father in the same household. This configuration, unfortunately is less than 30 percent. Girls may have parents who dropped out of high school, graduated from high school, earned a GED instead of a high school diploma, or earned an associate, bachelor's, or graduate degree. When you combine income, parental education, the 17 different types of parenting arrangements, and the four parenting styles (authoritative, authoritarian, etc.), the lives of Black girls become increasingly complex. Clearly they are not being raised in just one parenting modality. There are numerous ways that Black girls are being reared. While writing this book, I heard news reports about two White lesbians who wanted to raise a child. One wanted to be inseminated with white sperm. Incorrectly, she received sperm from a Black male. She gave birth to a biracial girl. They are now having difficulty with her hair and the racial comments they are receiving from their White neighbors. They have sued the clinic. My concern is for the girl.

Housing, Neighborhoods and Family Life

Another factor that impacts the lives of Black girls is the community in which they live. Not all neighborhoods are created equally. A neighborhood might include:

- Homeless shelters
- Inner city
- Outer city
- Suburbs
- Rural
- Apartment (rental)
- Apartment (condo)
- Townhome

Chapter 4: Demographics

- House: 1,000 square feet; 2,000 square feet; 3,000+ square feet
- Private bedroom, shared bedroom, no bedroom
- Safe neighborhood, dangerous neighborhood
- Food desert; few oases of healthy restaurants and grocery stores

Let's look at a couple of scenarios. One girl lives in an upper-income household, and the family income is more than $75,000 per year. Her two biological parents live in the same 4,000 square foot house. They live in a gated suburban community, and each child has her own bedroom. Both parents have graduate degrees, and their parenting style is authoritative.

The second girl lives below the poverty line. She is being raised in an institution in a dangerous inner city community where there are no good quality grocery stores. Her caregivers have less than a high school diploma, and their parenting style is mostly negligent.

And of course there are girls who live in situations between those two extremes.

Throughout my 40-year career, both professionals and lay people alike have tried to convince me that poor Black students from single-parent homes and whose parents lack degrees will never thrive academically or prosper financially in America.

Raising Black Girls

I want to dedicate this chapter to Rashema Melson. For two years, Rashema has been living in Washington, DC's largest homeless shelter at DC General Hospital, along with her mother and two siblings. The family's home life has been unstable for at least six years. Regardless of the challenges and instability of Melson's life, she has managed to produce a 4.0 GPA and secured a full scholarship to Georgetown University.

While some people may think that a homeless high school student may find it difficult to keep up with her studies, Melson said that staying motivated to succeed academically was easy for her because success is her life's goal.

"It's not hard for me because I want to," said Melson. "Like when you don't want it and you're just doing it because you have to, it's like a struggle. But I want to be successful." Melson also used her unfortunate circumstances as inspiration to do her best. "It's pushing me to be better, to know what I want in life, and to know this is *not* what I want, but I have to go through it for the moment."

I would love for all Black girls to live in an upper-income household with both biological parents, in a large house with a private bedroom, with parents possessing both graduate degrees and an authoritative parenting style, but I know many will not experience that. But if they have Rashema Melson's drive and motivation, if they can just have one adult who encourages, motivates, and serves as a positive role model, then Black girls can reach their full potential.

Before going on to the next chapter on mothers, I'd like you to take the following quiz. Please honestly grade yourself between and A and F. I also want you to share your grades with your daughter and see if she confirms your grades.

Grades

_____ Have you taught your children about God, His Word and the power of prayer?

_____ Do your children have goals?

_____ Do you provide quality time?

_____ Do you praise more than you criticize?

_____ How well do you listen to your children?

_____ Are you consistent?

_____ Do you give them high expectations?

_____ Do you teach your children African history?

_____ Have you provided your children with a nutritious diet?

_____ Do you monitor homework?

_____ Do you select, discuss and monitor television shows?

_____ Do you know your children's friends and their values?

_____ Could your children develop a family tree?

_____ Do your children receive adequate sleep?

_____ Do you take your children on field trips?

_____ How frequently do you visit your child's school?

_____ Do you listen and discuss your children's music selections?

_____ How disciplined are your children?

_____ How well do your children complete chores?

_____ How frequently do you touch your children?

_____ Have you provided a safe environment for your children?

Goal Setting

Have you set goals for your daughter? What would you like for her to achieve in school and in life?

I'm offering the following chart as a way to get you started on setting goals for your daughter. Really think about the goals you desire for your daughter, and write down different goals as you see fit.

What is your plan for achieving those goals? For example, it's easy to say, "I want my daughter to be an A student." But if there are no restrictions on television, music, and mobile devices, and if you are not checking homework *every night*, she probably will not achieve that goal.

GOALS	STRATEGIES/PLANS OF ACTION
Relationship with God	
Grade point average	
ACT/SAT test scores	
Dress size	
Athletic participation	
Cultural consciousness	
Integrity/respectful/kind/manners/generous	
Mate selection	
Friend selection	
Financial stability/inheritance/insurance	
Work ethic	

Let's now move into the next chapter on mothers.

Chapter 5: Mothers

This chapter is dedicated to Wanda Pratt. She is the mother of the NBA superstar Kevin Durant of the Oklahoma City Thunder. In 2014, he was voted MVP of the League. When he was giving his acceptance speech, he talked about his mother. "She raised my brother and I by herself. She worked two jobs. When there was only a little food to eat, my brother and I ate first, and many nights she went to bed hungry." He said, "My mother, Wanda Pratt, is the MVP."[3]

I also want to dedicate this chapter to Sara Gibbs. A single woman who worked long hours as a nurse, one day she made a decision that would change her life forever. Gibbs thought she would never be a mother, but after an infant girl was left on the doorstep of a nearby doctor's office, she made the decision to adopt the child. She's been raising Janessa ever since, all as a single mother working 12-hour night shifts.

"There was nothing in my life that had prepared me to be a mother." Janessa is now 18 years of age and headed off to college this fall.

When asked about her adoptive mother, Janessa said, "She's the best mom ever. She's always been there for me."[4]

Unfortunately, not all mothers are like Wanda and Sara. There are some permissive and neglectful mothers. A four-year-old daughter went into her mother's purse and thought she found several bags of candy. She passed them out to several students in her class. She did not realize they were bags of heroin.[5]

More than 90 percent of Black mothers stay with their children.[6] Two-thirds of Black girls say the person who has the greatest influence on their lives is Mama. I wonder about the remaining one-third. Who is influencing them? Their fathers? Grandparents? Other relatives? A teacher? Their friends?

Mothers love hard, and especially their daughters. They see themselves in their daughters. How does it feel to parent someone who looks like you? How does it feel to raise someone who reminds you so much of yourself at 5, 7, 10, 12, 14, 16 years of age? No relationship is more passionate, volatile, and rewarding than that between a mother and daughter.

Are you parenting by yourself, with the father, in a blended family, with your parent(s), with other relatives, or with another woman? What type of parenting style do you possess? Is it authoritative, authoritarian, permissive, or neglectful? Be honest with these questions because your daughter's future lies in your answers.

Parental Communication and Style

Did your parents ever tell you, "I hope you have a daughter who acts just like you." Are you finding that the following are creating conflict in your relationship with your daughter?

- Clothes
- Hairstyles
- Makeup
- Jewelry
- Bedroom
- Friends
- Music
- Social media

Chapter 5: Mothers

- Television
- Dating
- Chores
- Academics
- Truth
- Trust

A teacher once told me that he was concerned about the way one of his female students dressed. He thought her clothes were too provocative, too tight, too short, too revealing. He sent her home and said that in order for her to return to class, her mother needed to pay him a visit. The next day, the mother came to the school. She entered his classroom dressed exactly like her daughter had dressed the day before. The teacher took one look at the mother and understood the origin of the problem.

There's no relationship more passionate, volatile, or rewarding than the mother-daughter relationship. For many mothers and daughters, there's a lot of eye rolling, neck jerking backward and forward, hands on hips, and the favorite phrase, "Whatever!"

I'd like to dissect two questions that were on the quiz. The first concerns the power of words and praise. Parents need to understand the power of words. You can literally destroy your child with your words. Proverbs 18:21 says, "Death and life are in the power of the tongue." Words can cut sharper than a knife. A parent can say something to a daughter at five years of age that may still hurt her at 50. It hurts me to hear a mother curse her daughter and minutes later think she can remove the pain with a hug and a slice of dessert.

What is the ratio between your praise and criticism? Some mothers have a 0:6 ratio between praise and criticism. They seldom praise, and they criticize often. A 0:6 ratio of praise to criticism could destroy the child. The least we could do with our daughters is have a 1:1 ratio, where for every criticism given, words of encouragement and praise are given.

If you want to produce a superstar, if you want to produce a very accomplished and secure daughter, the ideal ratio is 3:1—three praises to one criticism. What is your ratio? Ask your daughter what she thinks the ratio is in your home. Is it 0:6, 1:1, or 3:1?

The next topic from the quiz which I want to explore is how well you listen to your daughter. Many times when someone is speaking, we are thinking about what we are going to say next. Good parents are effective listeners. They actively listen. They listen to not only what's being said, they listen to the heart and feeling behind the words. Because girls are very emotional, it behooves mothers to not only listen to what they are saying; listen to the emotions, feeling, and heart behind the words.

In my review of the literature on parenting, I found no more significant variable than the quality of conversation in the home. What are you and your daughter talking about at home? Are you talking about her future goals?

There's a big difference between asking, "How was school today?" and "What did you do in school today? Start with first period and walk me through each period of the day." You may receive only a one-word reply to the first question. It's better to ask the second question because it requires a detailed answer. Make sure you listen carefully.

When daughters know that the most important part of the conversation is about them and what they think and feel, they thrive and blossom. Girls need to feel important. Mothers need to convince their daughters that they are the most important part of their lives. In the earlier chapter on trends, I reported that 67 percent of females report sadness, depression and hopelessness that lasted up to two weeks. It is crucial that mothers and all caregivers listen to their daughters and also consider what is not being said. Caregivers should not be the last to know their daughter is depressed.

Chapter 5: Mothers

Listed below are some common reasons girls suffer from depression:

- Rape
- Incest
- Fatherlessness
- Divorce
- Loss of a loved one
- Witnessing a homicide or violent act
- Poverty
- Homelessness
- Bullying
- Breaking up with a boyfriend
- Lack of communication with parents
- Poor grades
- Neighborhood violence
- Sexual pressure from boyfriend
- Physical abuse
- Emotional abuse
- Dietary
- Chemical imbalance
- Female drama
- Social media
- Low self-esteem due to White standards of good hair, pretty eyes, slender facial features, lighter hue, and body weight.

Two of the most important factors in the parenting dynamic are trust and truthful communication. Can you trust your daughter? Does your daughter tell you the truth? It is very unfortunate when you can't trust your daughter and you don't know for sure if she's telling you the truth. Integrity must be taught during the toddler years. It is more difficult to teach trust and truthful communication when your daughter is a teenager. The sooner you teach your daughter to tell you the truth, the better. If you don't do anything else with your daughter, please make sure that you can trust her and that you can count on her to tell you the truth.

The best way to make sure she learns these two traits is to always tell your daughter the truth; in other words, be a trustworthy parent. Truth and trust should be reciprocal between mothers and daughters.

Truth and trust, or the lack thereof, will cause major problems in any relationship, and especially the one between mothers and daughters. Another source of contention are clothes, makeup, and jewelry.

Some mothers literally threaten their daughters with, "If you wear my clothes again, if you use my makeup again, if you wear my jewelry again, you're going to have to leave this house." What's been your experience between you and your daughter on clothes, makeup, and jewelry? Do you handle these issues from an authoritative, authoritarian, permissive, or neglectful perspective? The quiz asked if you're consistently authoritative, authoritarian, permissive, or neglectful. Daughters become confused when you have one rule on Monday, another on Wednesday, and another on Friday.

Do you model the type of dress and clothing style that you want your daughter to wear? Ironically, some mothers use their daughters' clothes, makeup, and jewelry. They like what their daughters are wearing more than the items in their own closets. Some mothers absolutely refuse to dress modestly. How can such mothers tell their daughters to tone it down when they dress so provocatively themselves?

About Men and Family Responsibilities

What are you teaching your daughter about men? What are you teaching your daughter about her father, who may or may not be present? Some women are angry at the fathers of their daughters. Some mothers are angry at Black men in general. Please do not destroy the relationship your daughter could have with her father or a man because of your bitter and historical feelings.

In the movie *Comeback Dad* starring Charles Dutton, the mother and father had divorced. The father sent letters to his daughter every month, but the daughter never responded. She hated her father. She was so angry at him. She thought her father didn't love her. It turned out that she never responded to her dad because she never received the letters. Her mother never gave them to her.

Mothers, are you teaching your daughter how to love their fathers and Black men? Or are you teaching her to hate her father and Black men?

Are you teaching your daughter how to make it with or without a man?

What lesson did you teach your daughter when you allowed your boyfriend to spend the night or move in?

Words are powerful. Have you ever told your daughter that all men are dogs? Men cannot be trusted? Always keep some mad money on the side? Be prepared for him to leave? Or are you teaching your daughter how to say no and when it's time to say yes with confidence?

Now let's take a look at household chores. Have you turned your daughter into your nanny, babysitter, maid, and cook?

I am all in favor of daughters learning responsibility. Every child needs to do chores. They need to know how to make up a bed, clean a house, do laundry, sew, iron, and cook. The problem is when a parent absolves herself from the parenting process and puts that burden on a child, thus stealing her childhood. Is your daughter raising your children? Please be honest.

Do you love your daughter unconditionally? Does your daughter know you love her unconditionally?

Are you trying to live your life through your daughter?

Are you helping your daughter develop goals? One of the questions on the quiz was related to goals. Can your daughter give a different career for each letter of the alphabet (excluding sports and entertainment)? Ask her to do this.

Have you expanded her borders? Have you taken her all over the city? Have you taken her to a play, museum, art gallery, an opera, or the zoo? Have you taken her across the state, country, and world?

Have you shown her the finer things in life? Have you taken her to a five-star restaurant? Have you taken her to a five-star hotel? Have you shown her luxury houses?

Tough Love Parenting

One of the hardest things for a mother to accept is that you can't protect your daughter from falling down. You can't protect her from making mistakes. You can't protect her from falling off her bicycle. You can't protect her from falling when she's roller skating or ice skating. You can't protect her from bullies in the neighborhood or in the classroom. You can't protect her from boyfriends who break up with her and treat her disrespectfully.

Tell your daughter, "You will make mistakes, but let's avoid the big ones, like teen pregnancy, STDs, and crime."

As a parent, you need to know that you have taught your daughter right from wrong. Too many girls are in prison. Too many females are in prison because they were holding their boyfriends' guns or drugs. Your daughter needs to know that this is a big one. It's one thing to fall off your bicycle. It's another thing to become pregnant at 13 years old or incarcerated before your 18th birthday. You need to have long, hard, intense conversations with your daughter about the big ones. I encourage you and daughter to read about Kemba Smith who was incarcerated holding her boyfriend's drugs.

There was a powerful scene in the movie *Middle of Nowhere*. The mother was at the dining room table with her daughter, and the daughter was experiencing low self-esteem. The mother knew she had raised her daughter better than that. She told her in no uncertain terms, "Hold your head up!" We need to make sure we are raising our daughters with their heads held high.

Chapter 5: Mothers

In my book *Educating Black Girls,* I reported that Black girls are scoring 17.1 on the ACT and boys are scoring 16.8. Why are girls only scoring .3 of a point above boys on the ACT and yet, as mentioned in the Trends chapter, girls' college graduation rate is 45 percent, but for males it's only 33 percent? Young women earn 66 percent of all associate, bachelor's and graduate degrees. I just don't think that .3 of a point explains that. I don't believe that schools K–12 deserve any of the credit for the tremendous performance that we are observing among Black females at the collegiate level.

How do we explain it? Well, some mothers are much harder on their daughters than their sons. They demand more from their daughters. As a result, girls are more goal oriented, focused, organized, and responsible. A girl knows that the time is waning on how long she can stay in her mother's house and wear her clothes, makeup, and jewelry. Unfortunately, there are some 40 year-old males who haven't learned that lesson, and they remain in their mother's house forever.

Young women perform much better at the collegiate level than males because their mothers served as excellent role models. Their mothers taught them how to be organized, responsible, motivated, and goal oriented. I commend mothers for the fantastic job they have done with their daughters. Some mothers have raised their daughters and loved their sons.

There is no relationship more passionate or more volatile than the relationship between mother and daughter. There is also no relationship more rewarding. Mothers, raising daughters is a very demanding job that lasts 24 hours a day, 7 days a week for a minimum of 18 to 21 years. Parents receive no training or classes, nor do you take a test or earn a license.

What is the reward? It's having lunch and shopping with your grown daughter, looking across the table at the product of all your years of parenting, knowing you can trust her and that when she tells you things, she's telling you the truth. Can you imagine, there

Raising Black Girls

will come a day when she will listen to you and your dreams and goals. She may even surprise you and buy your clothes and pay for the meal!

For the first 18 to 21 years, you will have to hold steadfast and remember that you are her parent, not her friend. She has plenty of friends, but only one mother. After age 21, while you will always be her mother, now the two of you can become friends. There is no more rewarding experience than to see a mother and daughter become friends.

Chapter 6: Fathers

Fathers, are you raising your daughter by yourself, or with your wife, your daughter's stepmother, grandparents, uncle, aunt, sister, brother, or another man?

The media have been silent about the fact that almost 400,000 Black males are single parents.[7] I would love for television news programs to open, not with another murder or drug deal, but by showing a 25-year-old Black male braiding his daughter's hair in preparation for church. We could encourage more fathers to stay if they saw more of themselves in a positive light.

The National Center for Health Statistics provided an excellent study on the myth of the absent Black father.[8]

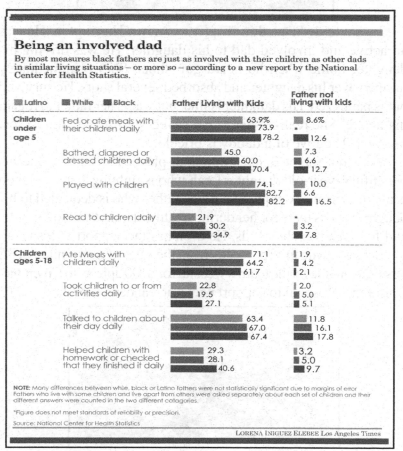

Being an involved dad

By most measures black fathers are just as involved with their children as other dads in similar living situations – or more so – according to a new report by the National Center for Health Statistics.

▪ Latino ▪ White ▪ Black		Father Living with Kids	Father not living with kids
Children under age 5	Fed or ate meals with their children daily	63.9% / 73.9 / 78.2	8.6% / * / 12.6
	Bathed, diapered or dressed children daily	45.0 / 60.0 / 70.4	7.3 / 6.6 / 12.7
	Played with children	74.1 / 82.7 / 82.2	10.0 / 6.6 / 16.5
	Read to children daily	21.9 / 30.2 / 34.9	* / 3.2 / 7.8
Children ages 5-18	Ate Meals with children daily	71.1 / 64.2 / 61.7	1.9 / 4.2 / 2.1
	Took children to or from activities daily	22.8 / 19.5 / 27.1	2.0 / 5.0 / 5.1
	Talked to children about their day daily	63.4 / 67.0 / 67.4	11.8 / 16.1 / 17.8
	Helped children with homework or checked that they finished it daily	29.3 / 28.1 / 40.6	3.2 / 5.0 / 9.7

NOTE: Many differences between white, black or Latino fathers were not statistically significant due to margins of error. Fathers who live with some children and live apart from others were asked separately about each set of children and their different answers were counted in the two different categories.

*Figure does not meet standards of reliability or precision.

Source: National Center for Health Statistics

LORENA INIGUEZ ELEBEE Los Angeles Times

47

Raising Black Girls

As you can see from the above chart, Black fathers are actively involved with their children from infancy to 18 years. Whether it's feeding them, eating meals together, bathing, changing diapers, dressing them, or reading with them, Black fathers are actively involved in their daughters' growth and development.

I want to dedicate this chapter to Shawn Harrington. He was an active and involved dad to his daughter. He was driving his daughter home when he heard gun shots. Shawn immediately jumped over his daughter and absorbed several shots. He survived but is paralyzed. His daughter is fine, but wants her father to regain his health. She realizes her father saved her life and almost lost his own. The love of a daddy is priceless.

Let's not forget Bengal's football player Devon Still and his beautiful 4-year-old daughter Leah who is fighting cancer. Devon is another prime example of a Black father who is dedicated to his daughter! He is there for her during treatments, shots, hospital visits and for whatever she needs. He even has the support of his team, the Bengels, who give proceeds from the sales of Still's number 75 jersey, available on the team's website for $100 apiece, to Cincinnati Children's Hospital to support pediatric cancer research.

Chapter 6: Fathers

In contrast to Shawn, Kelsey Smith became angry when his daughter soiled her diaper. First, he made her eat the waste from the diaper. He then proceeded to beat her to death.

I also want to acknowledge Kevin Jones. He is an excellent father to his 10 year –old daughter Janiya. His daughter is almost 6 feet tall and looks very mature. Janiya is on social media telling boys she is a teenager. Kevin did not approve of her social media involvement nor her lying about her age. Kevin decided to set the record straight and bought Janiya a t-shirt that says I am 10 years old.

Fathers, what is your parenting style: authoritative, authoritarian, permissive, or neglectful? Please be honest.

Second, review the quiz presented in Chapter 4. What grade did you receive in each of those categories? Please share your grades with your daughter for final confirmation.

Finally, look at the goals section at the end of Chapter 4, and remember, you are not restricted by the goals on the sheet. What goals do you have for your daughter? What plans and strategies do you have in place to help her achieve those goals?

Fathers, you must also honestly assess your praise to criticism ratio. Do you criticize more than you praise? Is there an equal ratio between praise and criticism? Or do you praise more than you criticize? Is your ratio of praise to criticism 0:6, 1:1, or 3:1? How well do you monitor the words you use with your daughter?

Raising Black Girls

Have you ever directed a derogatory comment at your daughter? Have you ever cursed your daughter? Have you ever hurt your daughter's self-esteem with your words?

Do you talk more than listen? There's a good chance you will lose your daughter if you don't listen to her. It is a tragedy and a travesty that a girl's friends will know more about her secrets, desires, and aspirations than her father.

The most important developmental factor in a girl's life is not the number of parents in the home, their income, or educational background, but the quality of the conversation that takes place at home. What do the two of you talk about? How often do you talk about her future? Have you shared your goals with your daughter?

Fathers are often reticent about spending quality time with their children when they're young. For example, some fathers erroneously believe that children belong with the mother from infancy to nine years and with the father after that. Many fathers do not fight for joint custody when children are younger. The discomfort men feel toward their daughters can be even more pronounced during puberty, when her body is beginning to develop.

The beautiful thing about your daughter is that she will teach you how to father her. She will show you what she wants to do with you. She will direct your conversation. Like dancing, just listen to her and follow her lead. She will help you develop a beautiful relationship with her.

There are six types of fathers:

1. **Sperm donors** feel their major responsibility as a father is to make the baby. While that may take as little as 18 seconds, sperm donors disappear for the next 18 years. Unfortunately, there are too many sperm donors in the Black community.

2. **No show daddies** promise their daughters on Monday they're going to pick them up Saturday morning and take them on an outing, but they don't show. Earlier, we mentioned that more than 90 percent of mothers stay with their children. Some men are so selfish and self-centered that when they break up with their exes, they break up with the children, too. Some mothers say that even when they ask the fathers to stay present in their

children's lives, they vacillate or flat out refuse. They simply disappear. I just want a father to explain to me how they do that. How do you divorce your child? How do you spend more time and money with your blended children than you do with your biological children?

3. **Ice cream daddies** feel guilty because they know they're not spending enough time with their children. So to rid themselves of the guilt, when they do take their daughters out, they buy them whatever they want. This is quintessential ice cream daddy, or sugar daddy, behavior.

4. **Stepdaddies** is a term I really hate. How can the man who stayed, is paying bills, and checking homework every night be called "step" and the sperm donor is called "daddy?" We need to reevaluate our terms. Step is a Eurocentric term that reflects a hierarchical, multi-tiered value system regarding relationships. In the African value system, however, there is no stepfather. In the village there are only fathers.

5. **Divorced daddies** are regulated by their ex-wives. They have to pay to play. Often they are denied access to their children based on their custody payments. In some cases, the father might be current on payments, but the mother still denies the father an opportunity to spend time with the children. I've had so many conversations with men in tears. They sincerely want to spend time with their children, but they've been denied.

6. **Daddies** never left their children. They've been with them every night since infancy. They nurture, encourage, listen and provide for their children.

Review these six types of fathers and ask yourself, "Which type am I?"

There are numerous ills in the Black community, such as racism, classism, and unemployment. One of the most significant ills is fatherlessness. Many studies have found that the most important factor impacting a child's life is not race or family income, but fatherlessness. A father is the most important man in his daughter's life. She will learn how a man is to love her from you.

Raising Black Girls

Listed below are some consequences of fatherlessness:
- Low grade point average
- Poor school attendance
- Retention
- Suspensions
- Special education
- Remedial reading
- Dropping out
- Promiscuity
- Teen pregnancy
- Abortion
- Gangs
- Crime
- Running away from home
- Alcoholism, drug addiction
- Incarceration
- Depression
- Suicide

If fathers only knew how significant they are in the lives of their daughters, they would never leave them. Many girls are suffering from fatherlessness. Many of our daughters are having daddy issues. Listed below are some of the issues our daughters experience when their fathers are not present or actively involved in their growth and development:
- They select bad men.
- They select thugs over nerds.
- They stay in bad relationships.
- They select significantly older men.
- They have multiple sex partners.
- They are in constant need of male affection and attention.
- They always cling to men.
- They accept verbal, emotional, and physical abuse from men.
- They can't trust men.
- They believe all men cheat.
- They believe all men lie.

- They believe men cannot keep a job.
- They believe men can't pay bills.
- They believe all men gamble.
- They believe all men use drugs and consume alcohol.
- They believe all men end up incarcerated.

One of the things I love about fathers who are actively involved in their daughters' growth and development is how they influence dating behaviors. Before the daughter goes out on a first date with a young man, a father expects to meet and interview him. His most important question is, "What are your intentions toward my daughter?" I love that fathers believe there will never be a man good enough for their daughters.

I also believe we need fathers to become more involved in their daughter's attire. Many girls are dressing very promiscuous. I believe the battle over attire should not rest solely on the mother. In addition, some mothers also dress provocatively. Daughters need their attire to be approved by their fathers.

Unfortunately, females say they experience sexual harassment in relationships 89 percent of the time. Sixty-one percent of the time there will be a physical altercation with a boyfriend.[9] Fathers must teach their daughters how to defend themselves through martial arts. It is imperative that fathers teach their daughters to be princesses and queens and to have strong self-esteem, keep their heads up, have high expectations, and never settle for relationships that are not rewarding, respectful, and complimentary.

Before we close this chapter, there are four additional points that I want to make to fathers.

1. Expand your daughter's borders and boundaries. Take her out of her neighborhood, and take her on a field trip downtown. Take her to the finest restaurant and hotel. Show her luxury homes. Show her the possibilities that are available to her. So many of our daughters have never left their neighborhoods. They've only been to fast food restaurants, and they've never been to a five-star hotel. They've never seen a mansion other than on *106 & Park.*

Raising Black Girls

2. Set limits for your daughter. It's not just the mother's job to discuss your daughter's clothing, makeup, and jewelry. If fathers would hold their daughters accountable on family rules, including dress code, the selection of friends and boyfriends, curfew, and media viewing, we would see more responsible behaviors in our daughters. Too many mothers are bearing this burden by themselves. Fathers often seem oblivious to the importance of setting and consistently enforcing limits. Please remember, your daughter does not need you to be her friend. She needs you to be her father.

3. You cannot protect your daughter from making mistakes. You can't protect her from falling down, losing her balance on her bicycle and roller skates, being bullied in school, friends not liking her, being teased over her dress, hairstyle, and hue. Accept that there are limits as to how far your protection can go, but stress to your daughter that some mistakes are more costly than others. You must do everything in your power to protect your daughter from becoming pregnant before she's ready or getting involved in criminal activity. Some mistakes are simply too costly.

4. On the greatest day of your daughter's life, one man will give her away, and she will marry the other. Ideally, she will spend the rest of her life with him. If you have done your job successfully, you will walk your daughter down the aisle, your little girl who was once in a car seat and who now asks you for the car keys. You will walk your princess down the aisle, and you will give your daughter away to the man you interviewed and approved. You will give your daughter away to him, and you will let her know in no uncertain terms that she cannot run back home when she doesn't get her way. She can come home if she has been physically or verbally abused, but once you give her away at the altar, you're expecting her to know how to keep her marriage together. Fathers, the years go by fast; do everything you can to enjoy them and develop your princess into a queen.

Chapter 7: Self-Esteem

There's a war taking place between Black America and White America around the definition of beauty. What is good hair? What are pretty eyes? What is the connection between hue and beauty/self-esteem?

You will lose every war and battle if you're not cognizant of the fact that you are in a war, a fight, and a struggle. Parents, White America is trying to destroy the self-esteem of your daughters. An entire book could be written on the impact that racism, sexism, classism, colorism, and Post Traumatic Slavery Disorder (PTSD) have had on all of us, especially Black females. If your daughter cannot recognize and resist racism, sexism, classism, and colorism, it will be difficult for her to have high self-esteem. It is your responsibility to do whatever you can to protect and insulate your daughter from the onslaught.

Let me paint the picture by starting off with a quote from a mother who understands the war, struggle, and battle she's in for the self-esteem of her daughter:

> It literally takes my breath away. They are, simply, beautiful girls. I tell them this often. Not just because I believe it to the core, but because the world conspires to tell my babies different—to ingrain in their brain that something is wrong with their kinky hair and their juicy lips and their dark skin and their piercing brown eyes and their bubble butts and thick thighs and black girl goodness. I promise you, it feels like I'm guarding them from a tsunami of your ugly pronouncements; magazines and TV shows and popular radio and movies and all of the rest of pop culture insist on squeezing all

of us women into a ridiculously Eurocentric, blonde-haired, light-eyed standard of beauty, but good God, unless you're parenting a little Black girl, you have absolutely no earthly idea how exhausting it is to be media whipped for not being a white girl.[10]

I'd like for you to read that quote again and again and again, and not just the words, but the passion behind the words. This mother eloquently and passionately described how difficult it is to be Black in White America and to preserve self-esteem within a Eurocentric culture of beauty that literally negates African beauty. When you read it, listen to her heart.

After Lupita Nyong'o won the Academy Award for Best Supporting Actress for her role in *12 Years a Slave,* she went on to receive another award from *Essence* magazine. In her acceptance speech she said:

> I want to take this opportunity to talk about beauty. Black beauty. Dark beauty. I received a letter from a girl and I'd like to share just a small part of it with you. "Dear Lupita," it reads. "I think you're really lucky to be this black but yet this successful in Hollywood overnight. I was just about to buy Dencia's Whitenicious cream to lighten my skin when you appeared on the world map and saved me." . . . I remember a time when I too felt unbeautiful. I put on the TV and only saw pale skin. I got teased and taunted about my night-shaded skin, and my one prayer to God, the miracle worker, was that I would wake up lighter-skinned. The morning would come and I would be so excited about seeing my new skin that I would refuse to

look down at myself until I was in front of a mirror because I wanted to see my fair face first. And every day I experienced the same disappointment of being just as dark as I had been the day before. I tried to negotiate with God: I told him I would stop stealing sugar cubes at night if he gave me what I needed. I would listen to my mother's every word and never lose my school sweater again if he just made me a little lighter. But I guess God was unimpressed with my bargaining chips, because He never listened. And when I was a teenager my self-hate grew worse as you can imagine with adolescence. My mother reminded me often that she thought I was beautiful, but that was no consolation. She's my mother, of course she's supposed to think I'm beautiful. . . . And my mother again would say to me, "You can't eat beauty. It doesn't feed you." And these words plagued and bothered me; I didn't really understand them until finally I realized that beauty was not a thing that I could acquire or consume. It was something that I just had to be.[11]

Lupita also said, "When I was in second grade my teacher said "Where are you going to find a husband who wants someone as dark as you?". I want you to read Lupita's words over and over and over again, and not just her words, but the passion, agony, and strength behind her words. She describes what Black girls and women are experiencing daily as they try to be Black while living in White America.

I was very hurt when I heard about the suicide in April 2014 of Karyn Washington, founder of For Brown Girls. The painful passing of the 22-year-old advocate for dark skinned young women

Raising Black Girls

led to a serious reflection about the horrible impact that colorism has had on the African American community. The following is a response, posted online anonymously from another beautiful Black woman who also experienced colorism:

> I struggled with colorism more when I was little because I'm the darkest person in my family. My brother and sister are very light, and my extended family is very light as well, so I used to feel some kind of a way about looking different from everyone else but my mom consistently told me I was beautiful, smart, intelligent, etc., and she was really good at reinforcing positive ideas about dark girls.[12]

Karyn fully understood that it was going to be a struggle, a battle, a war to be Black in White America. We lost a brilliant young advocate for Black girls when she died.

Another young Black woman, a student struggling with colorism and racism in America, said:

> All my life I have either been a minority or an outcast. In elementary school I was one out of three black children in the class, and I learned from a young age that I was different. I always had to wear my hair in French braids and wondered why other girls would have their hair flow freely and naturally. I would even cover my nose sometimes, embarrassed that it was broader than everyone else's. . . . Other races don't find me as beautiful because of my hair and darker shade of skin. I feel like people are watching me more closely and expecting me to do something wrong because apparently "I'm black and grew up in the hood." I

don't want to hate myself. I don't want to hate something I could never change about myself. I think it's stupid, yet the feelings are still there.[13]

I am reminded of the brilliant entertainer, Patti LaBelle, who once said, "I regret that I had cosmetic surgery on my nose. It was a painful surgery, and it was unnecessary. But back then, when I didn't know any better, when I hated how broad my nose was, I felt the only way to be beautiful was to have cosmetic surgery."[14]

Whoopi Goldberg once shared some comments that came from her mother. Her mother said, "Child, you're not the prettiest girl in the world, nor are you the ugliest. But because you're not as pretty as this world would have you to be, you're going to have to work twice as hard. You're going to have to be the best. You're going to have to overcompensate the lack of good looks."[15]

The brilliant and award winning actress Viola Davis has struggled with colorism her entire life. In response to the opening episode of the TV series *How to Get Away with Murder,* writers from the *New York Times* and *People* magazine tweeted Viola is "less classically beautiful", a fancy way of say they think she's ugly. Viola responded," I have been beautiful my entire life."[16]

In 1947, Kenneth and Mamie Clark used the doll test to ascertain how Black children felt about themselves, their hair texture, hue, and features. The researchers documented that Black children consistently chose dolls that did not look like them. They felt the White doll was prettier, looked better, and seemed smarter. That was in 1947, and the study was used to support the victory of *Brown v. Topeka* in 1954.[17]

Between 1954 and the present, some 60 years later, we still haven't gotten it right. In 2010, CNN hired Dr. Margaret Beale Spencer, a leading researcher in the field of child development, to repeat the doll study. Unfortunately, in the new study, Spencer found that Black children still selected the White dolls. Why? They felt the White dolls looked better and seemed smarter.[18] It is unfortunate that 60+ years after the original doll study and *Brown v. Topeka*, Black children still prefer dolls that do not look like them. I am not surprised at these findings.

Colorism and racism have been present in the entertainment industry for a long time, but even by Hollywood's racist standards, a casting call in 2014 seeking females to appear in a film about the Compton rap group NWA was truly disgusting. The directors wanted females with light skin to fill the "fine" girl roles and females with dark skin to fill the unattractive girl roles. The following casting call was posted via Gawker.

> *A GIRLS: These are the hottest of the hottest. Models. MUST have real hair – no extensions, very classy looking, great bodies. You can be light skin black, white, asian, hispanic, mid eastern, or mixed race too. Age 18-30.*
>
> *B GIRLS: These are fine girls, long natural hair, really nice bodies. Small waists, nice hips. You should be light-skinned. Beyoncé is a prototype here. Age 18-30.*
>
> *C GIRLS: These are African American girls, medium to light skinned with a weave. Age 18-30.*
>
> *D GIRLS: These are African American girls. Poor, not in good shape. Medium to dark skin tone. Age 18-30.[19]*

You would think the casting director was shooting a movie set in the early 1900s, not the present. But racism and colorism have been consistently present, and until African Americans are willing to acknowledge that we are in a fight and are willing to fight the battle, we will continue to lose.

Our daughters deserve better than this.

The Hue Advantage

While American workers would like to believe that their earnings are based on merit, effort, and determination, in reality, this is just not true. The Huffington Post recently reported that physical appearance has a significant and tangible impact on earnings. The findings, revealed in a video released by Box, compared earnings for those who are considered conventionally attractive and those who are not. When factors for age, family structure, job, and tenure were controlled, attractive and unattractive people were separated by a lifetime pay gap of $230,000. Studies show that people who are considered beautiful are generally seen as being more competent, kind, and trustworthy.[20]

Researchers Murguia, Telles, Hughes, and Hertel found similar patterns of inequality based on skin color stratification in school settings. They found that the education gap between Whites and Blacks was nearly identical to the education gap between light skinned Blacks and dark skinned Blacks.[21] As a consultant to school districts, I have observed thousands of classrooms where light skinned children sit in the front and dark skinned children sit in the rear, where teachers call on light skinned children more often than they call on dark skinned children. They encourage and give more feedback to light skinned children than dark skinned children.

This is not 1914, this is the present, yet racism and colorism are alive and well. Remember, colorism and PTSD are also executed by African Americans. Our response to racism and White male supremacy has been an internal hatred that is expressed in a myriad of ways.

This problem of how to be Black while living in White America transcends American boundaries. Our brothers and sisters in Africa, the Caribbean, Central and South America, and

Raising Black Girls

Europe are also having major challenges with the White Eurocentric definition of beauty. These messages have led to a booming market and availability of skin bleaching products in Africa and throughout the Diaspora. According to the World Health Organization (WHO), Nigeria has the world's highest percentage of women using skin lightening products at 77 percent. In Togo, the estimate is around 59 percent. The skin bleaching industry is valued at $150 billion.[22]

We know that slavery led to a collective and traumatic loss of self-esteem among Africans throughout the Diaspora, and it continues today. Listed below are some negative comments I have heard over the years.

- She's pretty to be so black.
- Can you pass the brown bag test?
- I'm glad she did not come out too dark.
- You stayed in the oven too long.
- Damn, you ugly.
- You black b**.
- She has good hair.
- She has pretty eyes.
- Is your hair straight as a ruler?
- She has a good grade of hair.
- Does your hair blow?
- I need to put bleach in the bathwater to get lighter.
- Don't get mad because I'm lighter than you.
- She thinks she's something with that pointed nose.
- My boyfriend left me for a high yellow girl.
- My boyfriend left me for a White girl.
- Don't marry Black.
- Rub the black off of you, girl!
- Your skin is dirty.
- I want to marry light to have pretty babies.
- I dreamed I woke up lighter.
- Tar baby.

- You wear white for weddings and black for funerals.
- Dark girls are just good for sex.
- Don't play in the sun to avoid being dark.

I'm reminded of the powerful book by Toni Morrison, *The Bluest Eye*. One of the main characters, Pecola, drinks white milk, hoping she will turn into Shirley Temple.

When our girls are given a regular dose of these negative comments, when they are exposed to a Eurocentric definition of beauty, they become real clear on where they are in the pecking order. It's difficult to convince a girl that she's beautiful when her classroom is ruled by a color-based, beauty-based pecking order. Ask your daughter if she knows where she is in the pecking order. In a classroom of, say, 30 students, 15 of whom are girls, where does she rank among the 15 in the beauty pecking order? It is a sad commentary that even in kindergarten, little girls know where they are in the classroom pecking order.

I want parents and caregivers to understand the seriousness of this situation. Despite your encouraging comments, your daughters are being persuaded by her *perceived* place in the pecking order.

Parents, I encourage you to teach your daughters their history and culture, and you should start before the year 1620. We need to start our girls on pyramids, not plantations. They need to know there was a time when Africans did not bleach their skin. Before the European invasions into Africa, our God looked like us and *not* Michelangelo's cousin. Before the Middle Passage, slavery, and European imperialism in Africa, dolls looked like us, and we liked how we looked. The standard of beauty was Lupita, Whoopi, and India Arie.

But with the invasions came control of the media, which was largely responsible for establishing the Eurocentric definition of beauty and color power around the world. It's one thing for Europeans to make God look like them for *their* children, but why did they have to make God look like them for *our* children? Why did Barbie become the definition of beauty? With her odd body shape, she even undermines the self-esteem of White girls.

As a result, the media—MTV, BET, Hollywood, New York's 5th Avenue, magazines, newspapers—have defined for our girls what it means to be beautiful. Beyoncé, Alicia Keys, Tyra Banks, and Halle Berry are the standard bearers of African American beauty. Please don't misquote me. I have nothing against these women. They have had no control over how their images are used by the media. The problem is that not all Black girls look like them. What is the future for the girls who do not look like them? Can girls who do not look like them have a healthy dose of self-esteem? How do we help them? How do we teach dark skinned girls with short hair and broad features that they are beautiful? That becomes the billion dollar question.

So many dark-skinned girls have been teased and bullied by female and male classmates and unfortunately their teachers. Ninety percent of beauty is between the ears. It's an inside job. Therefore we must monitor the images promoted in magazines, newspapers, and television, on billboards and the Internet that are bombarding our girls on a daily basis. Second, we must give our girls positive words of encouragement. We've read the negative quotes. Listed below are some positive comments that you can use to develop and reinforce your daughter's self-esteem.

- Tell your daughter every day that she's beautiful. Tell her until she believes it.
- The blacker the berry, the sweeter the juice.
- Teach your daughter the four benefits of dark skin:
  - It delays the aging process. You could have two women, one White, one Black, same age. But they will not look the same.
  - There's less chance of skin cancer.
  - There's less chance of sunburn.

- The darker you are, the more melanin you have. The more melanin you have, the more sun you can absorb. The more sun you can absorb, the more vitamin D you produce, and you need vitamin D for brain cell development.
- The late Maya Angelou said, "I am a woman, a phenomenal woman."
- Oprah Winfrey says, "Excellence is the best way to overcome racism, sexism, classism, and colorism."
- It's not what you call me, but what I answer to.
- I want you to dream big.
- You are worth more than that.
- You have too much to lose.
- You are beautiful to the one person that matters: *you!*
- I've never seen an ugly smiling face.
- Confidence is the sexiest thing a woman can possess.
- The question is not, "Who's going to let me?" It's, "Who is going to stop me?"
- Never underestimate the power of a woman.

Next, I want you and your daughter to watch the documentary, *Dark Girls*. It is a powerful film with some significant lessons. Every girl needs to see this documentary. I also encourage you and your daughter to watch the speech Lupita Nyong'o gave when she accepted the *Essence* award.

Weekly, watch *106 & Park* together. I'm not an advocate of the show, but our young males and females watch it. They're being taught a Eurocentric standard of beauty without the benefit of an adult's wise, culturally informed perspective. Our girls are being brainwashed without our supervision. Transform *106 & Park* into a lesson on history, culture, Eurocentric standards of beauty, positive vs. negative rap lyrics, and self-esteem.

Raising Black Girls

Since our girls love dolls, support the increasing number of Black doll companies that are launching into the marketplace. We didn't have Black doll companies in 1947. In 2010 when the CNN study was done, we had them, but the companies were not strongly marketed or supported. I encourage you to support the following companies:

- Natural Girls United
- Positively Perfect Dolls
- HIA Toys
- Uzuri Kid Kidz
- Kwanzaa Kidz
- EthiDolls
- Dolls Like Me

The Issue of Esteem
I'd like to you to ask your daughter the following four questions:
1. Who am I?
2. What is my purpose?

Chapter 7: Self-Esteem

3. On a 1–10 beauty scale, with 10 being most beautiful, where am I?
4. Do I have self-esteem, peer-esteem, or mate-esteem?

Let's probe the issue of esteem. Many girls value more what their boyfriends think of them than what they think of themselves. This is mate-esteem. If your boyfriend wants you lighter with longer hair and blue eyes and showing more body, what are you going to do? Are you going to avoid the sun? Avoid exercising? Are you going to use a lightening cream? Are you going to buy a weave? Are you going to purchase tinted contact lenses? Are you going to wear more provocative clothing? There is an inverse relationship between self-esteem and mate-esteem. Many of our girls, unfortunately, have low self-esteem and high mate-esteem. However, if your self-esteem is higher than your mate-esteem, you will not bow down to the dictates of your boyfriend.

The same applies to peer-esteem. If you value more what your friends think of you than what you think of yourself, then you have high peer-esteem but low self-esteem.

You will lose the war for your daughter's self-esteem if you fail to understand that she is the target of a fierce battle, and the prize is her soul. Let me be clear. White America is trying to teach your daughter to hate herself. She is learning that the only way to be beautiful is with light skin, long hair, and light eyes. If you are going to win this war, it will take more than a physical response. Putting weave in your toddler's hair will not build her self-esteem. Ephesians 6:12 is clear: "We struggle not against flesh and blood but against principalities and rulers in high places." We must bind the demons that are trying to entice our daughters to hate themselves. We must teach them that they are fearfully and wonderfully made.

Now, if parents do not like the way *they* look, if they value more what their mates and friends think of them, and if they do not believe they are fearfully and wonderfully made, then our daughters will continue to be confused and self-hating. It will take a village to teach dark and brown skinned girls with short, natural hair and broad features that they are beautiful. This village should consist of Africentric parents, caregivers, educators, churches, organizations, and media. If the Eurocentric village is stronger and more influential, we must fight even harder for the restoration of their souls and self-esteem.

In the next chapter, we will look at how issues related to hair impact our parenting and our daughters' view of themselves.

Chapter 8: Hair

I could write an entire book on the significance of Black hair and the impact it has made on the psyche of Black women in particular as well as the larger Black community. I encourage you to read books like *Cornrows, I Love My Hair!, Happy to Be Nappy,* and *Nappy Hair* to your children. Parents and caregivers should read books written for adults such as *Hair Story, Better Than Good Hair, If You Love It, It Will Grow, The Science of Black Hair,* and *Going Natural.*

Have your children watch *I Love My Hair,* a *Sesame Street* video you can view on YouTube. Chris Rock's movie *Good Hair* was a revelation.

I could almost call this chapter, "The Decision"—whether your daughter will keep her hair natural or have it processed. Or I could have called this chapter "64 Percent," because 64 percent of Black females (actually down from 74 percent over the past few years), have made the decision to process their hair.[23]

Also important is *when* the decision is made. In researching this book, I was flabbergasted to find that some parents give kiddie perms to their babies at *11 months old,* one year old, when the daughter enters kindergarten, or at the beginning of fourth grade. Some parents use the onset of menstruation to begin processing hair, like a rite of passage. By the time our girls have graduated from eighth grade, most of them have processed hair. Only a handful will start when they enter high school. For some reason, the gateway years are 8-11.[24]

Often, parents don't want to start perming hair, but when their daughters complain about being teased and bullied in school, they give in. I have talked to girls and read numerous stories about little girls as young as eight and nine years old, in third and fourth grades, being harassed by their classmates to get their hair processed. Parents give in, and because having it professionally done is so expensive, mothers buy the kits and do it themselves.

Raising Black Girls

That could cause further hair breaking, thinning, splitting, and falling out. Just try and imagine how devastated a young girl feels when her hair falls out. She was teased when her hair was natural, and now she's teased when her hair begins to fall out. She can't win.

I've even heard of girls transferring to another school just to avoid being harassed about their hair. It takes a village to raise a child, and ours does not, by and large, support natural hair. While there is a slowly growing natural hair movement among African American women, it hasn't quite filtered down to the grammar school and high school levels yet.

Imagine a young girl around eight years old. She's sitting in the salon or her mother's kitchen and receiving a kiddie perm. Her scalp is burning, and she's in severe pain. She cries, "Mama, mama! It hurts! It's burning!" Then she wipes away the tears and says, "I don't like my hair natural. I want it straight. I want to be like the other girls. Mama, I want my hair to look like your hair. I want my hair to look like the girls on the videos on *106 & Park*." I could write an entire book on what is happening psychologically as she sits in the chair, in tears, and at the tender age of eight years old. But at eight years she has decided that she would rather have her scalp burn and run the risk of her hair falling out than to keep her hair natural. Anything but that!

I'm reminded of the urban myth that says if you put bleach in your bathwater and sit in it for a while, you will become lighter. What if the myth were true? Soaking in bleach would really burn, but I wonder how many Black people would endure the pain just to become lighter?

I want to set the record straight on my position. I'm in no way implying that women with natural hair are more Africentric and politically conscious than those with processed hair. Hairstyles don't necessarily portray a person's values and commitment to the race. Many women wear different hairstyles for variety, convenience, or because 64 percent are doing it. It would be foolish to assume that anyone who has locks, braids, puffs, or a natural is

Chapter 8: Hair

Africentric, and anyone who has processed hair, wears a wig or a weave, or has her hair dyed blonde is Eurocentric and a sellout.

That said, I do believe that only neglectful and permissive parents would give a kiddie perm to an 11-month-old baby girl, toddler, or kindergartener. I just don't believe that an authoritative parent would impose this decision on a young child. Would you give a five-year-old child a car just because he wanted to drive? Of course not.

What is going on in the psyche of parents and caregivers as lye is applied to the tender scalps of their daughters? Do you think these parents do not love their daughters? I think they genuinely love their girls. In some cases, they made the decision *because* they loved them in their own interpretation of love. Some parents want to please their children. They want their children to like them. Their interpretation of love says, when you love someone, you give her things that she desires and likes so that you'll receive love in return.

Some parents say that they simply got tired. They conceded. Their daughter pestered them literally every day in kindergarten, first grade, and second grade, and finally, after days, weeks, months, and some years, they acquiesced and gave their daughter a kiddie perm.

Some parents say they gave in because other parents had given in to their daughters. This is known as the Everyone's Doing It syndrome. Children love convincing their parents that they need a thing because all their friends have this thing. She'll say, "I'm the only one in class with natural hair. It's just not fair!" This is why it's so important to belong to a village that will support your decisions.

I believe some parents made the decision to perm because they were lazy. They did not take the time to research the difference between heat damage and chemical damage. A hot comb or flat iron wouldn't have been great, but it would have been better than chemicalizing the life out of the child's hair. Even better, they could have used natural options like coconut oil, olive oil, Curly

Q's, Kinky Curly Kids, and Carol's Daughter Princess Collection to protect, condition, and smooth out the hair. They could have creatively braided, cornrowed, puffed, locked, or twisted the hair for variety.

Parenting is a 24-hour, 7 days a week, 18-year responsibility. Daughters are always watching their mothers. Mother is her most important role model. How could you convince your daughter not to have her hair processed when you, her most significant role model, has her hair processed?

The reality is, parents are going to perm their daughters' hair for whatever their personal reasons. That's why I am encouraging you to give this book to as many permissive and neglectful parents as you possibly can.

Personally, I believe that giving babies, toddlers, and young children perms, making them endure scalp burn and pain, borders on child abuse. I encourage you to Google the article, "When Kiddie Perms Go Wrong." The article links to a powerful video about what happens to the scalp of Black girls when they get a kiddie perm. It describes in full detail hair falling out. Before it happens to your daughter, you should at least be fully informed of the risks.

There are many types of kiddie perms: Just for Me, Dream Kids, Beautiful Beginnings, Smooth Roots, Pretty and Silky, Kids Organic, Sof n' Free n' Pretty, etc. The reality is that kids' perms are just as dangerous as the perms used by adults. It's just a slower process.

Perms contain a chemical called sodium hydroxide, which is lye. This is highly corrosive and breaks down the protein in hair. If left on the scalp too long or applied too often, it can cause bald spots. This chemical also permanently damages our lungs when inhaled, and this is just one example of the damaging properties of perms.

Have you ever wondered why Black women are three times more likely to experience uterine fibroid tumors? Beyond diet and obesity, a Boston University study found hair relaxers are a contributor.[25]

British scientists have discovered that some hair dyes used by millions of women have chemicals in them that have been linked to cancer.[26] It does not matter if you buy a hair dying kit yourself at the store or have it done at an expensive salon. When the dye comes in contact with tobacco smoke or other air pollutants, it has the ability to become toxic. Researchers say that one-third of women dye their hair.

Kiddie perms also use hydroxide, but rather than sodium, they use calcium. First, it's still a chemical. Second, it dries the hair and scalp more than sodium. This causes a greater chance for hair loss.

I want to commend Jasmine Lawrence who, at 11 years of age, created her own company, Eden Body Works. She was devastated by the damage harsh chemical products did to her hair. Jasmine sought to develop unique products that were all natural and really worked. Unlike most products that are cosmetic in nature, her mission was to develop hair care products that actually deliver on their promises. Eden Body Works has become a very profitable company. I encourage you to support Jasmine and purchase her products.

I also want to acknowledge Leanna Archer. This young lady started a profitable business by creating her own formula for hair care products designed to work with coarsely textured hair. Some women with thicker, harder to manage hair use quick fixes like oiling their scalps on a regular basis with natural oils like shea butter. She started a line of natural products targeted to African American women's unique hair textures. I encourage you to support Leanna Archer's products.

Extensions

There are at least four types of hair extensions and processes:

- Clip-ins – This is the easiest and cheapest way to add length and volume to your hair.
- Hot fusion or bonding – This is the most traditional way that hair extensions are placed in a person's hair. Your hairstylist will use a hot glue to fuse, or bond, the hair extensions to your natural hair.
- Cold fusion – This is a newer technology that is now being used because it's gentler on the hair than hot fusion. This method uses a keratin-based polymer to attach the extensions to the root of the natural hair.

- Weaves – A weave involves braiding the hair extensions into the natural hair. Many times a weave is more than just a few hair extensions, but will cover the entire head.

Many Black females want a weave, but cannot afford the price. They often go to an unprofessional who uses dirty utensils, cheap hair and hair pulled too tight. Unfortunately, this can cause irreparable damage to the scalp, infections and massive hair loss all for a few dollars saved.
Celebrities like Beyonce, Naomi Campbell, and Viola Davis and many other Black females are going bald due to dangerous hair weaves, extensions and chemicals. The condition is called alopecia. I encourage you and your daughter to research this condition.

Again, *why* are we making these decisions for our girls, and *when* are the decisions being made? Earlier, I mentioned that 64 percent of African American women have processed hair. Many women and girls tell me they process their hair because our culture, village, and media discourage them from keeping their hair natural. Interestingly, many also said that if their boyfriends valued natural hair, they would go natural, at least sometimes. They say Black males really love long, straight hair.

Listed below are some of the statements that women and girls shared with me.

- What is this, Mississippi burning day?
- I would leave the relaxer in longer to make it straighter, but it would burn.
- I know my mama loved me, but it burned my scalp, and her hot comb burned my ears.
- How soon can I straighten my hair to look like White girls?
- Kinky, not silky.

Raising Black Girls

- Thick, not thin.
- Black hair grows out. White hair grows down.
- If you can't afford to do your hair, hide it.
- When I see Black girls or women in braids, cornrows, or locks, it makes me think they look ghetto.
- Natural hair is unprofessional. Natural hair is okay for home, and processed hair is good for business and out at a nice function. Did you notice in *Scandal (first show of the 2014-2015 season)* when Kerry Washington was vacationing on the beach her hair was natural but when she returned to work it was relaxed?

In my book *Educating Black Girls,* I cited numerous examples of schools and school districts that suspended Black girls because their natural hair was in puffs, braids, twists, cornrows, and locks. Why should a Black girl be suspended because she wants to keep her hair natural? This is another illustration of racism and White supremacy. Not only do they control the media, but their schools mandate how our girls must style their hair in order to remain in school. This is yet another incentive for creating Africentric charter and private schools and homeschooling our children. We need a village that will support natural hair.

Remember when tennis stars Venus and Serena Williams began their careers in braids and beads? Not only did the media make this a big issue, but when beads fell off and onto the court, the Williams girls received a penalty. The authority said the beads violated "tennis etiquette." They went through an awful lot. These Black girls from Compton, who did not proceed through the accepted tennis regimen, were ridiculed. The girls chose not to participate in certain tournaments. They were coached by their father and not a certified coach, but look at the Williams sisters now!

Chapter 8: Hair

I'm reminded of the brilliant gymnast, Gabby Douglas. Here she is, winning the Olympic gold medal in gymnastics, and all the media wants to talk about is her hair, the bobby pins in her hair, her unprocessed hair, her natural, curly, kinky hair. Unfortunately, Black women participated in that awful discussion.

Many Black dancers and actresses have been told by their directors, "If you want to stay on the stage, you're going to have to do something with that nappy hair." How cruel, how insensitive in our "diverse, multicultural" society.

When people use terms like "culturally deprived," what they really mean is that they're so culturally arrogant that it's their way or the highway. If your hair doesn't look right to them, then you are culturally deprived. Thousands of Black women have been told by Corporate America, "If you want to get hired or keep your job in this company, you can't wear braids, locks, cornrows, puffs, or twists. The only acceptable hairstyle in this company is processed hair."

As I was writing this book, I was glad to hear that the U.S. military came to their senses and reversed their decision. After all these years of Black women being "allowed" to wear their hair natural, for a moment, the military tried to change the rules. There was such an outcry that the military decision makers returned to the original standard—cornrows, braids, twists, puffs, and locks. But it is still unfortunate that Black women had to fight to stay natural, and that the acceptable norm is processed hair while natural hair is considered abnormal.

There are numerous consequences of chemicalizing Black hair. Burning scalps, hair falling out, pain, and the possibility of lung cancer are only a few. For example, 40 percent of Black women do not exercise because they don't want their hair to "go back."[27] Go back where? To its natural state? Remember, with more than 40 percent of Black women either overweight or obese, it is imperative that all Black women exercise. How unfortunate that some women have chosen a hairstyle that they can't exercise with. Some females will exercise one day a week, and it will be the day right before they go to their hairstylist.

Seventy percent of Black women can't swim. That's a safety hazard. I wonder, is there any correlation between the 64 percent with relaxed hair and the 70 percent who can't swim?

I love taking advantage of steam rooms and saunas. Steam is healthy for the skin and good for the body. It relaxes you and reduces stress. But steam is not good for processed hair. So unfortunately, many Black women do not take advantage of steam rooms and saunas. Similarly, they're afraid to be caught outside in the rain or when the humidity is high.

Parents and caregivers must redefine good hair for Black girls from an Africentric perspective. We can no longer allow the White community and White culture to define for us what is good hair. All Black girls need to be taught that their hair is good. Good hair breathes and is not pulled too tightly around the edges. Good hair is alive, not burned or chemicalized to death. Good hair is chemical free. Did you know that perms stifle hair growth? Good hair is growing hair. Good hair allows you to do what you want to do when you want to do it. Good hair allows you to be free!

I'm reminded of the powerful lyrics from India Arie's 2006 song "I Am Not My Hair."

Little girl with the press and curl

Age eight I got a Jheri curl

Thirteen and I got a relaxer

I was a source of so much laughter

At fifteen when it all broke off

Eighteen and went all natural . . .

Chapter 8: Hair

I am not my hair

I am not this skin

I am not your expectations, no no

I am not my hair

I am not this skin

I am a soul that lives within.

So you and your daughter really need to sit down together and calmly have a heart to heart discussion about hair, yours and hers. Talk to her about the hair challenges you went through as a young girl, and even now as an adult. Discuss how hairstyles and choices connect to self-esteem, mate-esteem, and friend-esteem. Honestly ask yourself, "Was it my decision to wear my hair processed (or natural)? Did I make the decision because of my mate's likes and dislikes around hair?" If you've been challenged in this area, imagine how much more difficult it would be for a child.

Now ask your daughter:

- Does your boyfriend want your hair to be processed?
- Does your boyfriend think you're prettier when your hair is straight?
- Does your boyfriend think you're prettier when your hair is long?
- Does your boyfriend think your hair is prettier when it flows in the wind?
- Does your boyfriend think your hair is prettier when it's blonde?
- Do you value more what your boyfriend thinks than what you think? If so, you don't have self-esteem. You have mate-esteem.

Raising Black Girls

- Do you value more what your female friends think than what you think? If so, you have friend-esteem, not self-esteem.

Ask your daughter who's making the decisions about her hair. Is her self-esteem strong enough to withstand differences of opinion among her peers? Is she tough enough to make decisions for her and her alone?

In the next chapter, we will explore her academic challenges.

Chapter 9: Academics

I encourage you to read my book, *Educating Black Girls*. The entire book is devoted to the academic development of Black girls and was primarily written for educators. In this chapter, we will look at academics from the parent's vantage point.

Let's start with the positive stats.

- 2.4 million Black females are in college, 45 percent of whom will graduate.
- 66 percent of all associate's, bachelor's, and graduate degrees earned by African Americans are female.
- Many African American females earn GPAs higher than 3.0 in high school and college.
- Thousands of Black females are valedictorians of their high school and college classes.
- Thousands of Black females rank in the top 10 percent of their high school and college graduating classes.

Thousands of Black women attend Spelman, Bennett, and Smith (the largest female college in America). They also attend Harvard, Yale, Princeton, and all the colleges in between. Notice I led off with Spelman and Bennett, the only two Black colleges for females only. I encourage you to take your daughters to visit Spelman and Bennett.

Raising Black Girls

I want to dedicate this chapter to Kirstie and Kristie Bronner. They were the first twins to be co-valedictorians at Spelman. They both scored a perfect 4.0 GPA!

Now let's look at some of the negative stats.

- 82 percent of Black girls are below proficient in reading.
- 87 percent are below proficient in math.
- 21 percent are retained.
- 12 percent are suspended.
- 8 percent are expelled.
- 40 percent drop out.
- 2 percent of the doctors are Black females.[28]

First Lady Michelle Obama went to one of the best magnet schools in the city of Chicago, but she was told by her advisor that there was no need to apply to Princeton because she would not be admitted. Parents have to fight these types of negative comments. They must visit classrooms and hold teachers, counselors, and administrators accountable. If Michelle Obama had believed her counselor, she never would have applied to Princeton, graduated, applied to Harvard Law School, graduated, met President Obama, or had such a brilliant career. Michelle's entire life could have been destroyed by the words of a counselor. Parents, you must also monitor what *you* say to your children and how you say it. Let your words be filled with encouragement and high expectations.

In *Educating Black Girls,* I related the unfortunate story of Jada Williams, a brilliant student in Rochester, New York, who was asked to read a book about Frederick Douglass. She was moved by the book and Frederick Douglass' desire to read. He was beaten many times for reading. Jada made a correlation between the struggles of African Americans trying to read in the 1830s and African Americans trying to learn how to read in the 21st century. Her teacher did not approve of her analysis, and suspended her for making the correlation between modern day illiteracy and illiteracy in 1830.

Chapter 9: Academics

Twelve percent of Black girls are suspended. Why? Because they're critical thinkers like Jada, or they choose to wear their hair natural, or they're too loud, or any number of invalid reasons. Can you imagine being suspended because your hair is in puffs, cornrows, twists, locks, or braids?

Numerous Black girls are suspended because of their attitude, and teachers do not understand this issue from a cultural perspective. Isn't it interesting that White girls have strong leadership potential, but Black girls are too aggressive, assertive, and attitudinal? Can you imagine hundreds of Black girls being suspended because they rolled their eyes at a teacher, put their hands on their hips, and moved their necks? Teachers feel this behavior is belligerent and defiant. Yes, we must teach our girls how to debate and communicate respectfully, but we should also strive to understand the source of this behavior. We must help our daughters with impulse and emotional control. Attitude can come from high or low self-esteem. It depends on the girl and what she's going through in life. If teachers, and parents for that matter, would take the time to understand where the attitude is coming from and not take it personally, they could take measures to diffuse the tension on the spot.

Allow me to share another horror story with you. Salecia Johnson was a kindergarten student at Creekside Elementary in Milledgeville, Georgia. She was having behavioral problems in school, and the teacher did not know how to handle it. So the teacher and principal decided to call the police. That's right, they called the police on a little girl in kindergarten. The police came to the school, handcuffed Salecia, and placed her in a squad car by herself, without her parents, and took her to the police station. Then her parents were called to pick her up. This was not an isolated case. This has happened to numerous Black girls across the country.

At Sparkman Middle School in Toney, Alabama, the administration wanted to catch a boy who had been sexually abusing girls in the restroom. They decided to use a Black girl as bait.

Raising Black Girls

Their plan failed and she was raped. The family had to file a complaint with the Justice Department.

A Black girl at Oakleaf High School in Orange Park, Florida was publicly shamed because her skirt was too short. She was told she had to wear a sweat suit with the words Dress Code Violation.

Kendra Turner was raised in a strong Christian home. She was taught if someone sneezed to say, "God bless you." She was suspended by the teacher at Dyer County High School in Memphis for disrupting class.

Let me give the most typical scenario facing Black girls. Picture two girls, one Black and the other White. They are suspended for fighting each other. In many cases, the White girl is given a warning and the Black girl is suspended or expelled. In this case, they were both suspended and sent to an alternative school. For some strange reason (you fill in the blank) the White girl was allowed to return to the school after 90 days. The Black girl had to stay the entire year and she is now further behind academically as she returns to her original school.

I am reminded of *Brown v. Topeka* and how we thought African American life would get better with integration. Can you imagine, before 1954 and the first 20 years after that landmark decision, a Black teacher calling the police on a kindergarten child, and the child gets arrested? I wonder how many Black teachers and administrators would have called the police on a kindergarten child?

Could 1954 be the year that some Black people got what they wanted and lost what they had?

In another horror story, 17-year-old Omotayo Adeoye attended the prestigious Harlem High School for Math, Science and Engineering. While taking an exam, Adeoye's teacher caught her peeking at her phone. The teacher took the phone and began to scold her. A classmate recalled that the teacher began yelling, "You shouldn't be cheating. You guys shouldn't be cheating." Adeoye then began to cry and repeatedly apologized, but the instructor responded, "You are not really sorry. That's not a sincere apology." Later during the class period, Adeoye wrote a note on her test: "I just want to go away forever on the bottom of the river." She then asked to use the restroom and never returned. Adeoye walked away from her school to the Hudson River. According to WABC-TV in New York City, men who were fishing along the shoreline saw Adeoye place her belongings down, and then she jumped into the river. The men called for her to come back to shore, but to no avail. The men watched helplessly as her body sank under water.[29]

Successful Parenting

How can parents help their daughters succeed academically and psychologically so that they end up at Spelman, Bennett, Smith, Harvard, Yale, and Princeton rather than in a watery grave?

Successful parents know that academic success is *not* based on the number of parents in the home or their income level or their educational background. I just love it when, despite the odds, African American parents somehow, someway, get all their children into college, and all children graduate. Do you think that happened by accident? How can a single parent with eight children produce eight college graduates? That was not luck. That just doesn't happen. That takes effort, a plan, a program.

Academic conversations. Parents and caregivers, what are your goals and the plan to achieve those goals to produce academic excellence in your daughters? Successful parents make academics the number one priority in their households. It is the number one topic of conversation. Research shows that the most important variable in producing a scholar is the quality of conversation in the home.[30]

Expectations. It has been said that in Asian homes, if grades are lower than an A, changes will be made. There will be less television, video games, music, and playing outside. In White homes, anything lower than a B, changes will be made. But it is said that in Black homes, as long as the child passes with a C, there's no need for changes.

Are Cs acceptable in your household? What are your expectations for your daughter? Is your daughter aware of your expectations?

Television. We all know that television is like a thief in the day and night, robbing our children of their time, thoughts, and values. Later, we will look at television in more detail, but for now I'd like you to assess your rules around television watching. Can your girls watch as many hours as they want? Are they allowed to watch TV every day? Can they watch whatever they want to watch? Successful parents have rules around television. What are your television rules?

Reading. In high achieving homes, reading is a daily activity. Parents read to their children in the womb. From infancy to the first day of kindergarten, they continue to read to their children and have their children read back to them. The achievement gap does not start in eighth grade. It starts early. Some children enter kindergarten with more than 20,000 hours of a book in their hands. Other children start with less than 20 hours of a book in their hands. Anyone who knows me and the work I've done as a consultant to school districts knows that I'm very critical and hard on educators, but I can't blame this on them. Who had the children before the first day of kindergarten? Not the teachers. This is a parental issue.

Summer vacation. Research shows there's a three-year academic achievement gap between White and Black students. One reason for the gap is that some Black and White students spend their three-month summer vacations differently. Some students read books, visit libraries, museums, and local colleges. They stay academically engaged. Other students sleep longer, watch more television, play more video games, play outside more, listen to more music, but seldom, if ever, do they read a book.

The formula below explains the three-year gap.

3 (months) x 12 (grades 1–12) = 36 (months)

Chapter 9: Academics

There's the three-year gap between Black and White students. The gap will be closed quickly when parents create, and enforce, an academic plan for the summer months. But if your children do nothing else, insist that they read for at least an hour every day. They should also write for an hour every day. Both skills, reading and writing, are fundamental to school success.

Home environment. If you want to produce a scholar, entrepreneur, or STEM (science, technology, engineering, math) genius, there are certain things you will need in your home. Rappers, ball players, and thugs need certain things in their homes. When I see more CDs and music downloads than books/e-books, I'm concerned. Do you have a microscope, telescope, chemistry set, e-book reader, and/or a computer in your home for your children? Does your home environment reflect your high expectations?

African Americans often say the reason they don't have these essential learning tools is because they are too expensive. Yet these same parents have several pairs of Air Jordans in their closets. It is said that Black people buy what they want and beg for what they need. Successful parents prioritize spending based on their goals and aspirations for their children.

STEM

Raising Black Girls

I want to acknowledge the great work of Ayanna Howard. She is a brilliant roboticist and professor of electrical and computer engineering in Atlanta. She is also a leading researcher in her field. I am concerned about the paucity of Black women in the medical and STEM fields. Only two percent of the doctors in America are African American females. I'd like for you to share with your daughter the following: secretaries earn an average of $24,000 per year; engineers average $155,000 per year; and doctors average $250,000 per year.

Expose your daughter to science toys and programs between infancy and nine years of age. We're losing large numbers of female engineers and doctors, not in high school, but in the primary and intermediate grades. We need to expose our daughters to science as early as possible. Several toy companies are emerging to plant seeds and inspire girls to study these subjects. You can do your own search online, but following are a few recommendations:

- **GoldieBlox** (www.goldieblox.com) – Offers toys that are attractive to girls and encourages them to pursue careers in engineering and construction.
- **Roominate** (www.roominatetoy.com) – Uses dollhouses to encourage girls to pursue careers in math and science.
- **Sabotage at the Space Station** (http://smartadventures games.com) – S.M.A.R.T. Adventures™ math games use fun concepts to help girls attain STEM literacy and confidence at every stage in their educational career.
- **SciGirls** (http://scigirlsconnect.org) – Excellent science resource for girls.

There's a movement afloat, largely dominated by White women, designed to encourage their daughters to pursue STEM. Black girls and their parents need to take advantage of this movement. There's a certain mind-set you'll have to adopt, however, to help your daughter along. Let's look at how two families address this issue.

Chapter 9: Academics

One girl receives an airplane that is already put together. She has no appreciation of its engineering or the work that it took to create and build. As a result, the daughter throws the plane across the room, and the plane breaks. Soon her parents are off to the store to buy another toy.

The second girl receives a plane kit with 150 parts from her authoritative parents. They assist the daughter, but ultimately she has to do most of the work. It takes more than a couple of hours to put this plane together, maybe several days or weeks. The daughter is learning perseverance, engineering skills, and fortitude, and she is developing a strong work ethic. Several hours, days, or weeks later, all 150 pieces have been assembled. She paints the plane and decorates it with decals. You can be assured that this girl will not throw her plane across the room because she appreciates the time and effort she took to build it.

What types of toys do you buy for your daughter? Are they pre-made, or do they require assembling? I encourage you to take advantage of this movement for your daughter's sake, and support the companies mentioned above.

Traditional toy stores haven't really caught up with the times. It's so disappointing to see the segregation of toys along gender lines. It's like we're back in the 1920s—pink for girls, blue for boys; dolls for girls, construction tools for boys. Our society continues to groom boys into STEM and girls into fine arts and language arts when *all* children should have a healthy dose of both.

Advocate on behalf of your child to have her placed into AP (advanced placement), honors, gifted and talented, and IB (International Baccalaureate) classes. She may be the only African American in the class, so her self-esteem must be strong enough to withstand being the focus of attention. Is your daughter's self-esteem strong enough? Can she handle insensitive White students making these kinds of asinine statements?

- You're different.
- You don't sound Black.

- You don't act Black.
- Can I touch your hair?
- Why do Blacks sit together in the cafeteria?

Is she able to handle insensitive racist teachers who ignore her when she raises her hand? Can she handle knowing that her teachers do not expect as much out of her as her White classmates? What if she never receives encouragement or feedback from her White teachers? Can she handle it? Your daughter will probably be seen as the resident expert of all African American issues in the classroom, so when the subject of slavery comes up, all eyes will turn to her. Can she handle it?

Are you willing to sit in on her classes and monitor her teachers?

Expectations

Could it be that girls are less influenced by bling bling? Do girls believe they have less chance of going pro in the WNBA than boys in the NBA? Do girls believe they have less chance of becoming a successful rapper, while boys believe they have a greater chance of becoming the next Jay-Z or 50 Cent? Could it be that girls believe they have less of a chance of becoming the first female drug dealer who will not get caught while boys believe they will be the first drug dealer who will not get caught?

In the next chapter, we will look at the impact peer pressure has on your daughter.

Chapter 10: Peer Pressure

Greatest Influences on Youth

1980:

home
school
church

Present:

peer pressure
music
television
social media

There's a rumor that the peer group is the number one influence on your daughter. Is that true?

Is the peer group raising your daughter?

Does your daughter value what her friends think more than what you think?

Are our girls following the advice of their peer group more than the advice of their parents?

There is a direct relationship between age and peer pressure. As age increases, so does peer pressure. Parents, you must become aware of what's going on with your daughter's friends, and you must do everything possible to reduce the influence of peer pressure on your daughter's values, attitudes, and behaviors.

Unfortunately, many adolescents believe their parents are not as smart as their peer group. Yet, when they become older and reach their '20s, when they become a mother with children, then their parents become smart again. During adolescence, when girls need their parents the most, they rely on them the least.

You may think your daughter is an angel, but if you really want to know your daughter—her values, morals, beliefs, likes, and dislikes—all you have to do is observe her selection of friends. Do you know the names of your daughter's three best friends? Ask your daughter to name her three best friends. Did you get the names right? Then ask her why she chose those girls to be her best friends. Invite your daughter's friends over to get to know them better.

Does your daughter know the difference between a friend and an associate? Does she know what a fake friend is? Does she know that a friend will not lie on her, will not gossip about her, will honor and respect the relationship she has with her boyfriend? A friend will encourage you. She will fight for you. A friend has your back. She would not forward your photo over the Internet without your permission. Ask your daughter again about her three friends. Do these three people encourage her and honor her relationship with her boyfriend? Will they fight for her? Will they tell her the truth even when she doesn't want to hear it? Do they have her back?

I decided to write a separate chapter on peer pressure because it's the number one influence on our girls. Peer pressure can determine your daughter's GPA. If your daughter chooses the wrong friends, if she chooses friends who do not value academics, if her friends associate being smart with acting White, if her friends do not aspire to be in gifted and talented, honors, AP, and IB classes, that will affect her GPA. You may be doing your job in encouraging academic success, but the peer group could be working against you.

Her choice of friends could determine if she goes to college, or which college she attends—a junior college, business college, state college, Spelman, Bennett, Smith, Harvard, Yale, or Princeton.

Her friends determine what type of music she prefers. If her friends like gangster rap and they're okay with rappers calling them out of their names, your daughter will probably gravitate toward this type of music.

Chapter 10: Peer Pressure

Girls do not participate in sports for a myriad of reasons. It would be nice if your daughter's friends loved and valued athletics. Not only would she be persuaded to get into a sport, but through sports she would develop skills, sports*woman*ship, the ability to work with a team, discipline, physical stamina, and weight management. Mastering a sport would build self-confidence and self-esteem. All this could rest with her choice of friends.

Your daughter's friends are probably determining what she watches on television. She could have one group of friends who values watching more scholarly shows on television, shows that have a message and are educationally driven, or another group of friends might persuade her to watch shows that are, bottom line, a big waste of time. Some of these Black reality shows feature females who fight, curse, and abuse one another. That's not good for her moral, psychological, or spiritual development.

She could choose a group of friends who do not curse, or she could run with a group of friends who curse like sailors. One set of friends might dress modestly, but another dresses very provocatively.

Some of your daughter's friends might value natural hair; others may have been getting their hair processed since kindergarten. One set wears little to no makeup, while the others have makeup caked all over their faces. She could choose friends who want boyfriends, and older boyfriends at that, or she could choose friends who have decided to wait.

One day three girls went into a department store to steal some clothes. Two girls were on lookout while the other girl tried to steal three blouses, one for each girl. Can you imagine going to jail over a blouse? Could your daughter have been one of those three girls? Are you absolutely sure your daughter is strong enough to resist her peer group when they are up to no good?

Parents, if you don't do anything else, you need to know your daughter's friends. You need to know how your daughter is handling peer pressure.

I'd like for you to share these quotes with your daughter.

- Show me your friends, and I will show you your future.
- The key to failure is trying to please everyone.

- I am not in this world to do what you want me to do.
- Some go with the flow, and others go against it.
- "Everybody is doing it" is an excuse, not a reason.

Most, if not all, parents have heard their children say at least once, "Everybody is doing it." Permissive and neglectful parents fall for the okeydoke. They allow their daughters to do things they know is not right, but because their daughters have convinced them that "everybody is doing it," and they can't possibly allow their daughters to be isolated and alone, neglectful and permissive parents succumb to the pressure.

Authoritative and authoritarian parents remind their daughters, "Your friends don't live here. They don't pay the bills. They are not responsible for your growth and development. Until they are paying the rent and the utilities and all the other expenses, then you will do what *I* say."

Have an honest discussion with your daughter about whether or not her friends really have her back. What if she was pregnant (God forbid) and gave birth to the child. Ask her to consider the following:

- How much time would her friends spend with her?
- Would her friends help wash the clothes?
- Would they change diapers?
- Would they babysit so she could go to a party?
- How much time would her friends spend helping her raise her child?
- How do her friends feel about abortion?

Ask your daughter, "If you were hospitalized or at home ill for 30 days or more, how much time would your friends spend visiting you and nursing you back to health?"

Last, but not least, ask your daughter, "If you were incarcerated, how many times would your friends visit you while you were in prison?"

In the next chapter, we will look at the impact of music on our daughters.

Chapter 11: Music

Greatest Influences on Youth

1980:

home
school
church

Present:

peer pressure
music
television
social media

There's a rumor that singers and rappers have the greatest influence on your daughter.

There's a rumor that singers and rappers are raising your daughter.

There's a rumor that your daughter thinks she's only listening to the beat, when in reality, her brain computer has stored every lyric.

One of the major reasons why music has such a powerful influence on our daughters is that the average African American is listening to 2 hours and 33 minutes of music per day on their iPod or mobile device or watching music videos on TV or their laptop.[31] How many hours per day does your daughter listen to music? You think you know your daughter? Listen to her music. You think your daughter is an angel? Is she listening to angelical music? Do you really think your daughter can listen to gangster rap and not be influenced by it? Does your daughter believe she is a queen or a b**? Is she listening to queen music or b** music? The type of music you listen to not only lets me know what you think of yourself, it will determine and shape your values.

If you want to understand what entertainers think of your daughter, listen to their music. If you want to assess the quality of male-female relationships, listen to their music. If you wonder why more than 50 percent of Black females are abused by their boyfriends, listen to their music.

Rap music has come under intense scrutiny because the lyrics and images promote some of the worst of society's ills. However, not all rap music is bad. Let me share with you some positive lyrics.

- "Come Close," Common: "Your whole being is beautiful / I'ma do the best I can do / because I'm the best when I'm with you."

- "Faithful," Common: "Faithful to thee / We got to be / … Baby you a blessin' and my best friend / That's what I'm gonna do / Faithful to the end / Faithful to thee / We got to be."

- "I Remember," Mary J. Blige: "I used to throw a fit, I used to shed a doubt / And blame it on a man but that was Mary then / And this is Mary now, you gotta understand / It's about how we respect ourselves / And the men have no control of our self-esteem / When we see that then we can let go / I remember."

- "Single Ladies," Beyoncé: "'Cause if you liked it then you should have put a ring on it / If you liked it then you should have put a ring on it / If you liked it then you should have put a ring on it / Don't be mad once you see that he want it / If you liked it then you should have put a ring on it."

- "Run the World (Girls)," Beyoncé: "Girls, we run this motha, GIRLS! / Who run the world? Girls! / Who run this motha? Girls! / Who run the world? Girls!"

- "Independent Woman," Destiny's Child: "All the women who are independent / Throw your hands up at me / All the honeys who makin' money / Throw your hands up at me / All the mommas who profit dollas / Throw your hands up at me / All the ladies who truly feel me / Throw your hands up at me."

- "Miss Independent," Ne-Yo: "Ooh it's somethin' about, just somethin' about the way she move / I can't figure it out / … Said ooh it's somethin' about kinda woman that want you but don't need you / I can't figure it out / There's somethin' about her, 'cause she walk like a boss, talk like a boss / Manicured nails to set the pedicure off / She's fly effortlessly / And she move like a boss, do what a boss do / She got me thinkin' about gettin' involved / That's the kinda girl I need."

- "Daughters," Nas, "How fathers feel for they daughters, / …When she date, we wait behind the door with the sawed off / Cuz we think no one is good enough for our daughters."

Is your daughter listening to positive lyrics? What does it say about your daughter if she's not listening to lyrics that empower, encourage, and inspire her? Following are some highly disturbing rap lyrics.

- "Confessions (Part 2)," Joe Budden: "Pray that she abort that / when she talk about keeping it. one shot to the stomach she leaking it."

- "P-Poppin," Ludacris: "Now pop that couchie you know the procedure / If you want this cash gotta make that a** shake like a seizure."

- "P.I.M.P.," 50 Cent: "I don't know what you heard about me / But a b** can't get a dollar outta me / No Cadillac, no perms, you can't see / That I'm a m**f** P.I.M.P." I also want you to watch this video. 50 Cent has two women on a dog leash.

- "Every Girl," Lil Wayne: "I like a long haired thick red bone / . . . I wish I could f** every girl in the world."

- "Successful," Trey Songz: "I want the money, money and the cars, cars and the clothes, / ...And even when the Phantom's leased them hoes wanna get in."
- "Every Girl," Young Money: "Open up her legs then filet mignon that p** / I'm a get in and on that p** / If she let me in I'm a own that p**."
- "Bottoms Up," Trey Songz: "If a b** try to get cute I'ma stomp her / Throw a lotta money at her then yell f** her."
- "Livin' It Up," Ja Rule: "I got a stick, I'll ride right next to you / Do a doughnut, and cut, and I'll open it up."
- "Splash Waterfalls," Ludacris: "You better not of came, she want to feel the pain."
- "The Next Episode," Dr. Dre and Snoop Dogg: "And if yo' a** get cracked, b** shut yo' trap."

The B Chart**

I'm reminded of the late, great Gil Scott-Heron, who said in one of his songs, "You can't call her a b** in one song and a queen in the other / Which one is she?" Unfortunately, it's as if rappers *must* call women b**'s and rhyme about b**'s. Apparently it's a hip hop law.

- Kanye, "Perfect B**"
- Dr. Dre, "B**s Ain't S**"
- Ice Cube, "A B** is a B**"
- Snoop Dogg, "I Don't Need a B**"
- Ludacris, "Move B**"
- 50 Cent, "Fat B**"

Are these rappers suffering from bipolar disorder? Is she a b** or a queen?

I want you to watch Nelly's video, "Tip Drill." In the video, Nelly swipes a credit card through the anus of a Black female. Spelman was so furious at Nelly that they refused to allow him to perform on their campus. You and your daughter need to have honest conversations about these rappers. Ask her if she can name five positive male rappers under 30 years old who are successful and making lots of money.

I don't blame hip hop and the rappers for sexism. Hip hop and the rappers did not create sexism. The rappers have nothing to do with the fact that Black women make $0.69 to every dollar that White men make. The rappers had nothing to do with the fact that women did not receive the right to vote until 1920. Rappers had nothing to do with sex trafficking and pornography, both of which are billion dollar industries.

Rappers simply want to get paid. In a country driven by capitalism, where the dollar is king, record labels have made it clear that if you want to be a clean, positive rapper and you want to call her a queen, then they will do very little to promote you. You will get little to no radio play, nor will you receive a lucrative contract. But if you call her a b**, if you disrespect her, if you violate her womanhood, they will pay you all the way to the bank.

The record labels promote misogyny, which is hatred and disdain of women. This is an ideology that reduces women to objects for men's ownership, use, and abuse.

Help your daughter and her friends organize a letter writing campaign to EMI, BMG, Sony, and Time-Warner, the companies that are funding and promoting this misogynistic culture and the radio advertisers. This activity will force them to study the lyrics, research names and addresses, and write persuasive copy.

It's ironic that for most of his career, Jay-Z had no problem calling women b**s, but now that he has a daughter, he's decided that he will no longer use the word. So, Jay-Z, it takes you having a daughter for you to realize the error of your ways? But what about all the other daughters of years past? Why didn't they matter?

This reminds me of all the males who have participated in sex trains. What if the female was their daughter, sister, or mother? How would they feel then? Maybe we need to make this issue more personal so, like Jay-Z, men will finally see the light.

I want you and your daughter to watch the video, "I Twerk for Jesus." Have a conversation with your daughter about twerking.

Raising Black Girls

Notice the smoothness of Satan. When you twerk for Jesus, I guess that makes twerking okay.

In some of the rap award programs on television, the rappers are poorly dressed and tattooed from forehead to ankles. When accepting an award for a rap CD that calls women outside of their names, many rappers will say, "I want to thank my Lord and Savior Jesus Christ for giving me the ability to earn this award." When Will Smith hosted an awards show, he called them out on this hypocrisy.

Once a week, watch *106 & Park* and *Sisterhood of Hip Hop*. Even negative shows can be turned into an educational moment if you are present. The problem has been that our daughters have been watching these reality shows and music videos without any adult supervision. That's what happens with permissive and neglectful parents. Authoritative and authoritarian parents are more hands on. They are determined to teach their daughters to think critically about the lyrics they hear and the images they see. These parents will not allow some rappers to undermine their daughters' self-esteem.

I would be remiss in a chapter on music if I did not include jumping rope. Almost every Black girl in America can jump rope. The beauty of Black girls jumping rope with such rhythm is fantastic. There are some schools that include this as competitive sport. Remember the lyrics, "Banana banana, banana split, What did you get in arithmetic?" Or what about, "I know something, but I won't tell, three little monkeys, in a peanut shell, one can read, and one can dance, and one has a hole in the seat of his pants." I would love for you and your daughter to jump rope and sing these songs together.

Lastly, I encourage you and your daughter to watch two positive documentaries: *The Souls of Black Girls* directed by Daphne Valerius and *Beyond Beats and Rhymes* written, produced and directed by Byron Hurt.

In the next chapter, we will look at the impact that television and social media have on our daughters.

Chapter 12: Television/Social Media

Greatest Influences on Youth

1980:

home
school
church

Present:

peer pressure
music
television
social media

I encourage you to read *The Kaiser Report: Generation M*^{2}.[31] We live in a "me too" society that is highly individualistic and self-centered. Notice the terms iPod, iPhone, iPad and iWatch. We live in an "I" society. Is your daughter self-centered? Is she selfish? How many selfies does she take? Does your daughter have an entitlement personality? The rumor is that television, the Internet, and social media are the greatest influences on your daughter's values, attitudes, and behaviors. Is your daughter being raised by television, the Internet, and social media?

The Kaiser Family Foundation reported that 70 percent of parents, probably neglectful and permissive parents, have no rules regarding how much television their daughters are allowed to watch. The average Black child is watching 5 hours and 54 minutes of television per day.[32] Do you have any rules regarding how much television your daughter can watch?

Raising Black Girls

Some parents allow their children to watch television in their bedrooms. The report stated that 71 percent of parents allow televisions in their children's bedrooms. Does your daughter have a TV in her room? Can you honestly say how many hours your daughter watches television in her bedroom with the remote under her pillow? When you went to sleep at 9:00 p.m. was she still awake and watching television?

In my opinion, the most important hour of the day for the family is the dinner hour. When your family has dinner together, and hopefully you do, are you also watching television? Earlier we discussed the importance of conversation. The dinner hour is the perfect time for family members to talk to one another. When the TV is on, however, there will be little conversation.

There is a strong correlation between grade point average and television watching. There's an inverse relationship. If television watching increases, GPA decreases.[33]

Race	SAT Scores	Time Spent Watching TV (per day)
Whites	1582	3 hours 33 minutes
African Americans	1291	5 hours 54 minutes

Successful parents monitor television. They have rules, such as "No television Sunday night through Thursday night." Some allow children to watch 30 minutes to an hour per night. I'm reminded of the great pediatric neurosurgeon, Dr. Ben Carson. His mother realized her sons were brilliant, so she decided to turn off the television during the week and made them read library books instead. There really is a correlation between television and grade point average. Unfortunately, 70 percent of parents have no rules at all.

Fifty percent of young people are watching television programs, not on a TV console, but on their mobile device, laptop, tablet, or PC.[34] What about your daughter? Is she watching television just on the console? An iPad? Another mobile device? Are you monitoring all devices?

What exactly are your children watching? *The Kaiser Report* shows that 54 percent of parents have no rules regarding what their children watch on television. Do you at least monitor what your daughter watches on television?

According to *The Kaiser Report,* 64 percent of all television programs feature sexual encounters.[35] Eighty percent of those encounters occur outside of marriage. Your daughter is watching 20,000 commercials per year that primarily promote sex.

Television has been pushing the profanity envelope for years, and on cable channels, no word is off limits. The only word on broadcast channels that is off limits is the f** word, and even that has been used.

By the age of 18, our daughters have observed 200,000 acts of violence and 40,000 murders. What is your daughter watching on television? Write down what you think are her top 10 television shows. Ideally you're watching those shows with her. Next, ask your daughter to list her top 10 shows. While television shows change from season to season, at the time of this writing, the following were the most popular TV shows for Black female youth:

- *Sisterhood of Hip Hop*
- *Love & Hip Hop*
- *Housewives of Atlanta*
- *Bad Girls Club*
- *Basketball Wives*
- *Scandal*
- *Dancing with the Stars*
- *106 & Park*
- *TI & Tiny*
- *Girlfriend Intervention*

The term "television" tells us that the industry is *telling* us their *vision* for you. They want to shape your world. The following chart is from *The Kaiser Report.*

Raising Black Girls

Descriptor	Media Portrayals of Black Youth (by percent)	Media Portrayals of White Youth (by percent)
Smart	32	84
Expected to succeed in life	21	88
Expected to fail in life	79	9
Players	87	32
Sexually aggressive	73	39
Irresponsible in romantic relationships	74	39
Happy in romantic relationships	30	71
Loyal in relationships	24	57

36

I don't know why any responsible parent would hand over her Black child to an industry that thinks like this about our youth. This media bias is as unacceptable as a police officer who shoots an unarmed Black youth who has his hands up and is saying, "Please, don't shoot!" These stats are psychologically violent. We cannot afford to expose our daughters and sons to media that think this way about our youth. Discuss the chart in full detail with your daughter.

Driven by capitalism and profits, television programmers believe the best way to portray Black youth on TV is as thugs, players, and hoes. We must monitor this industry. Can you imagine, we are willingly exposing our daughters to 5 hours and 54 minutes *daily* to programs that are biased *against* them.

Chapter 12: Television/Social Media

Mobile Devices and Social Media

Do you have any rules regarding your daughter's use of her mobile device? How many hours can she use it? When and where can she use it?

I've observed classrooms in which teachers allow their students to use their mobile devices, and not necessarily for academic reasons.

Where does your daughter charge her device? In authoritative and authoritarian homes, parents have rules such as, "By 9:00 all devices are in my bedroom to be charged." If you allow your daughter to charge her device in her bedroom, you'll have no idea when she stops using it (or *if* she stops using it). Kaiser found that the mobile device has become the average child's best friend. She spends:

- 33 minutes per day talking on her mobile device
- 49 minutes per day being exposed to other forms of media
- 17 minutes per day listening to music
- 17 minutes per day playing games
- 15 minutes per day watching television
- 90 minutes per day texting. That's 118 texts per day and more than 3,000 texts per month. I've even seen young people text each other at the same dinner table![37]

Is your daughter's mobile device the greatest influence on her life? Television and mobile devices have become the new drugs. Could your daughter, and even you, go without television or the mobile device for one day? Could you fast one day per week from television? You don't think it's a drug? Try it.

What about sexting? Most teens are comfortable with documenting their lives online, posting photos, and updating their status. Sending pictures and messages is problematic enough, but the real challenge comes when the content is shared broadly, as far too many teens have found out. The recipient of these messages is in possession of highly compromising images that can easily be posted on social networking sites and sent all over the world. Twenty-two percent of teen girls have sent nude or semi-nude photos of themselves over the Internet or their phones. Has your daughter ever sent a nude or highly suggestive photo of herself to anyone? I pray she never sends a nude photo.

Earlier, we talked about the distinction between a friend and an associate, a friend and a fake friend. If your daughter sends a compromising photo to her girlfriends, she runs the risk of her trust being violated. They may decide to send the photos worldwide. This happens even more when photos are sent to a boyfriend—and don't let the two break up. Your daughter needs to know that once she sends the photo, she loses control over her body. Unfortunately, in some situations, she sent her nude photo to a friend and someone else gained access to her mobile device and they made it viral.

There are numerous horror stories of girls who have sent photos of themselves in trust only to be violated. Now their friends at school, in the neighborhood, and the entire world have seen her in a compromising position. For some girls, the anguish and embarrassment was so great that they decided death would be better than to live under such conditions, and they committed suicide. Parents, please, have a conversation with your daughter so this will never happen to her.

The Internet

What are your daughter's favorite websites? Have you visited those websites? Do you have devices set in place to prevent your daughter from going to certain sites? Kaiser reports that 70 percent of parents monitor their children's online activity, and 46 percent have password access.[38] It's interesting that some parents are doing a better job monitoring the Internet than television. Parents need to monitor television, mobile devices, and the Internet. All three need to be in the 70 percent category. But, I commend those parents who are monitoring their children's online activity.

The unfortunate reality is that 70 percent of teens have found ways to hide their online activity. Many teens like visiting violent and porn sites. Has your daughter ever viewed pornographic sites? Has she ever participated in a chat room? Has she ever met a stranger from online activity? There are horror stories of girls "hooking up" with adult men they met in chat rooms and not living to see tomorrow.

Our daughters grow up so fast. A minute ago they were in the car seat. Now they're in the seatbelt. You need to protect your daughter's innocence and her childhood. Fifteen is not the new 11. Nineteen is not the new 15.

Please share with your daughter these two pledges written by the brilliant scholar and activist, Dr. Venus Evans-Winters.

BLACK GIRLS' MEDIA DECLARATION

The Parents **Pledge**

I AM A BLACK PARENT and I PLEDGE to do my part to protect the images of Black girls in media. I promise to monitor my daughter's online activities. I promise to report images of Black girls that involve sexual content or violence to the proper authorities. I promise not to expose my daughter(s) to visual images and music that are disrespectful to Black girls or women. I promise to promote and share positive images of Black girls with my social media network. I promise to teach my daughter(s) how to be safe online and how to use social media responsibly. I will teach my daughter(s) that there are consequences to her negatively presenting herself online that can potentially ruin her future or self-esteem.

Lovingly Signed

In the next chapter, we will look at the impact dating and sexuality have on our girls.

Chapter 13: Dating and Sexuality

This chapter really could be two books. There have been many books written just on dating and others just on sexuality. In this chapter, I will briefly look at both of them because of their similarities.

Have you ever had a conversation with your daughter about dating? Have you talked to her about what to look for in the selection of a mate? Is it possible that your daughter's friends are having the conversation about dating because you're not?

We do a better job selecting our cars, clothes, houses, and careers than we do selecting a mate. There really is a science to selecting the right mate. It is unfortunate that our daughters could have a 4.0 GPA, 1600 on the SAT, eventually receive their graduate degrees, and earn a six-figure salary, yet they were never taught by you how to select the right mate.

What good is it to have a degree, career with a six-figure salary, a mansion, and luxury car, but no one to share them with? What good is it to have all those things, but you go from one bad relationship to another?

One of the best gifts we can give our daughters is to teach them how to select the right mate. But parents and caregivers can't teach what they do not know. If they have not selected the right mate, if they don't know how to select the right mate, if they are not in a wholesome, fruitful, respectful relationship, it makes it more difficult to teach the science to their daughters.

When I listen to popular radio stations and they're playing the Mating Game, the top characteristics or traits that people say they're looking for in a mate are as follows:

- Good looks
- Intelligence
- Good sense of humor
- Likes to have a good time
- Wears nice clothes
- Cool

Raising Black Girls

The above describes practically everyone on the planet. Most people believe they look good, are intelligent, have a good sense of humor, like to have a good time, wear nice clothes, and are cool. That explains why so many of us have not done a good job selecting the right mate.

Many of us choose our mates based on chemistry, which connects to "looks good." Let me translate. Chemistry is the same as physical attraction.

Some of our girls like thugs. They like their men to be hard. They like men who can fight and protect them. They like players who have money, cars, and clothes. Listen to 50 Cent and Ciara's song, "I Can't Leave 'Em Alone" with your daughter. Ciara says, "I tried that good boy game / But the dope boy's turning me on."

Whitney Houston was a beautiful sister, brilliant singer, but she had a dark side—and it wasn't just Bobby Brown that was the problem. Whitney liked men like that. She gravitated to them. I've observed females on the honor roll in elementary school, high school, and college overlook the scholars and go after thugs and players. Could our daughters be choosing thugs because they are suffering from fatherlessness? Could their daddy be a thug? Fathers could really play a major role here in helping their daughters not to gravitate to thugs.

Our girls need help, and no one can help them more than their parents. We need to help our girls choose the right mates. They don't need to choose thugs. They deserve much better.

Has the influence of gangster rap affected your daughter's ability to choose the right mate? Would she overlook someone like Common and Ne-Yo and their lyrics and choose the disrespectful lyrics of a 50 Cent, Nelly, Snoop, Joe Budden, Trey Songz, Lil Wayne, Ludacris, Ja Rule, or Young Money?

Our society is so influenced by the external—good looks, "good" hair, "pretty" eyes, and "pretty" light skin. Have we been suckered into Hollywood's romantic notion of love? We think we should marry our lover rather than our best friend. You've heard the phrase, "Ain't nothing going on. We're just friends." How unfortunate that when we break up with our lovers, we pour out our hearts to our best friend. So why don't we see that best friend as mate material? Oh, that's right, no chemistry. It shows how we're socialized.

Please don't misquote me. I'm not saying you should date or marry an "ugly" best friend. What I am saying is that we should put more value on the internal. If the lack of communication leads to breakups and divorce, yet you enjoy communicating with your best friend, *duh!*, that's the one you should have chosen.

We must teach our daughters how to choose *good* men and not thugs. Can you imagine your daughter valuing a mate not based on his looks, but on his GPA, SAT score, and career goals; how well he listens to her and respects her decision to wait on sex; how well they study together at the library, do science projects together, and debate issues together. Now that's a relationship that could be fruitful and last a lifetime! I encourage you to have an honest conversation with your daughter about choosing a mate. Teach her how to tell the difference between a thug and a good male who shows potential.

Many of our girls are beginning to hang out or hook up in middle school. Often they are doing this without us being aware that they have a boyfriend. Notice, I did not use the word dating. Many youth and adults say dating is ancient. They say it requires too much structure. Boy must ask girl out and pay for the event. If we just hook up or hang out as a group, either one can ask the other to hang out, no one has to pay for the other and we can still check each other out. They like using the phrase, "friends with benefits."

It has been said that girls love hard, especially their first boyfriend. We need sensitive, caring parents who know how to listen to their daughters when they experience their first breakup. Parents and caregivers, not the peer group, need to be in the first position of influence to help our daughters through the pain. They really believed they were in love at 13 years old.

You can't protect your daughter from the pains she will experience. You can't protect her from selfish, mean males. But you can be a good listener. Help her so that her self-esteem is not broken beyond repair and that her self-worth is not dependent on a male. Perhaps your biggest challenge will be to resist making negative comments about men in general. This is not the time to berate men. That was one boyfriend. This is not the time to run your negative agenda that you may have about men, or her father. She's hurting about her particular boyfriend and what he did. You need to understand that and help her heal and learn from it and be ready to explore another relationship when she's ready. This is the time to help her understand what mistakes were made. What lessons can be learned through this experience? What can she do better the next time?

We always hear that opposites attract, but I don't believe that. Not at the gut level. I believe like attracts like. I'm always amazed at Black women who are critical of Black men and make disparaging comments about them. If a good Black man knocked on your door tonight, would you be ready? The best way to date is to prepare yourself so that when he knocks on your door, you'll be ready.

The same applies to your daughter. Study her and ask why she's consistently attracted to males who sag their pants, enjoy negative rap lyrics, speak negatively about females, use profanity, want her to change her appearance, or who abuse her verbally, emotionally, and physically. What does this say about your daughter's personality, self-esteem and self-worth?

Most important, if your daughter really loves the Lord, why would she choose a boyfriend who has no relationship with Him?

Chapter 13: Dating and Sexuality

Sexuality

First, we must talk to our daughters about their beautiful body and this includes their fathers. We must discuss every part of their body and its function. The sooner we start the better and we must take advantage of every teachable moment. I just love fathers and mothers talking about this issue when their daughters are in preschool or primary grades. Children are so inquisitive.

Why do you think Black girls start puberty on average at 8 years 8 months and White girls at 9 years 7 months? Could it be that Black girls receive less breast milk and consume more meat and processed food? What is the relationship between BMI (body mass index) and puberty/starting the menstrual cycle? Females start their menstrual cycle earlier based on BMI.[40]

Is your daughter psychologically ready to start her menstrual cycle away from you? In school? At some other location? Have you made the conversation fun? Have you told her that unlike males she receives a new cleansing every month which contributes to her longevity?

Today our girls are becoming sexually active as young as nine years old, but parents are not having the conversation until their mid- to late teens. Many parents are uncomfortable talking about sex with their daughters, and they end up having the conversation too late.

The National Campaign to Prevent Teen and Unplanned Pregnancy, together with *Essence* magazine, published the results of an excellent survey, "Under Pressure: What African-American Teens Aren't Telling You about Sex, Love, and Relationships." The report answers the very important question, "What keeps young people from talking to their parents about sexuality?"[41]

- 42 percent say it would be too awkward.
- 30 percent say they don't want parents asking too many questions.
- 23 percent don't know how to bring it up.

- 21 percent say they already know everything they need to know.
- 17 percent say they don't want their parents to be disappointed in them.
- 17 percent say they don't want their parents to know they've already had sex.
- 15 percent don't want their parents to tell them not to have sex.

Let's review these very important points. Is it too awkward for you to have a discussion with your daughter about sexuality? Is it possible that your daughter has been sexually active and does not want you to know? How would you respond if she told you she was sexually active?

The following comes from The National Campaign.

Considered Acceptable	By Family (percent)	By Friends (percent)
Sex during the teen years	28	68
Teen pregnancy	12	30
Teen parenthood	12	32
Having a baby outside of marriage	31	48

42

Is the peer group the number one influence on our youth? Well, 68 percent of friends believe it's okay to have sex during the teen years and only 28 percent of parents (probably neglectful and permissive).

Chapter 13: Dating and Sexuality

Friends believe 48 percent of the time that it's okay to have a baby outside of marriage. That's why it's imperative that parents regain their position as the primary influence on their children. Many youth tell me the only conversation their parents have about sex is to abstain. They believe that is not a conversation, but a commandment. Ironically, when females tell males no, they cynically ask what part of no did you not understand. Many parents say no, many females say no and most males say yes. We are talking but is anyone listening? Are daughters listening to their parents who are saying abstain? Are males listening to our daughters when they say no?

Let me now give some sexuality statistics.
- 1990: 100.3 teen pregnancies for Black females.
- Present: 43.9, a 51 percent decline in teen pregnancy.
- 70 percent of teenagers say that pregnancy right now would be a disaster.
- 67 percent of teens have had sex at least once without protection.
- 45 percent use birth control inconsistently.
- 32 percent have had sex with someone a lot older than they are. [43]

When I was in high school there was a freshman male who had a 3.5 GPA. He was dating a young lady with a 4.0 GPA. He wanted to be an engineer, and she wanted to be a doctor. They expected to be married after college. Because he was only a freshman and had no money he would visit her on his bicycle, the only transportation he could afford. When she became a sophomore at 15 years old, she met a young man who was 21 years. He had dropped out of school and was working in a factory. But he had a car. It was a piece of a car, but it was a car. She dropped her 15-year-old engineer and began going with the 21-year-old factory worker with a piece of a car.

Raising Black Girls

Remember, she wanted to be a doctor. She had a 4.0 GPA. She now has had six of his babies, and he is nowhere to be found. Please share this story with your daughter, as well as the following statistics:

- 1 out of 3 have had sex while drunk.
- 51 percent say there is pressure from society to have sex.
- 48 percent feel pressure from the media.
- 41 percent say their friends pressure them to have sex.
- 36 percent feel pressure from their boyfriend.
- 51 percent say it's embarrassing to admit being a virgin.
- 1 out of every 4 girls has an STD, and 48 percent of Black girls have an STD.
- Of the females who are HIV positive, 64 percent are African American.
- Many females complain about anal sex and the risk of an STD, but agree to satisfy their boyfriends.[44]

Parents, you must have conversations with your daughter about the above stats and trends. Each warrants an in-depth conversation, and feel free to use the following quotes when talking to your daughters:

- My body, my rules.
- Do you understand the word no?
- I don't until I say I do.
- You are more than the sum of your parts.
- Sex is not love.
- A baby will change your life forever.
- 18 seconds of sex can cost you 18 years of your life.
- If you believe your body is the only way to keep him, you don't have him.
- What is your sexual reputation?
- You don't need a baby to love yourself.

- Have you no shame?
- Have you no morals?
- A girl with no standards will fall for anything.
- Abortion is not birth control.

Give your daughter a budget sheet. Have her tell her boyfriend, "Before we have sex, I need to know if you can pay for rent, utilities, food, a car and insurance, telephone, cable, clothes, entertainment, and miscellaneous expenses." She should also say, "Before we have sex, you need to assure me that you can pay for all these items, because if I become pregnant we will need for all of these items to be paid."

BUDGET	
RENT	$1000
UTILITIES	$600
FOOD	$500
CAR	$1000
INSURANCE	$300
TELEPHONE	$100
CABLE	$100
CLOTHES	$200
ENTERTAINMENT	$200
MISC.	$200

Your daughter needs to know that pregnancy affects females differently than males. When pregnancy occurs, only the female body changes, not the male's body. Only the female gains weight, not the male. Only the female will miss days of school, not the male. When the baby is delivered, it will be the female who will sleep less. It will be the female who will be thinking about the child 24 hours a day, seven days a week. The mother's every decision will have to take the child into account. It's the female, not the male, who will miss basketball games, parties, and picnics.

Within the peer group, myths about sexuality are told and retold and they become almost like truths. Listed below are some of the popular myths that peers teach each other.

- Oral sex is not sex.

- Anal sex is not sex.

- I can be a virgin because I'm only involved in oral or anal sex.

- You can't get pregnant the first time.

- You can't get pregnant during the first three to six months of having sex.

- If you shower or douche within 30 minutes of ejaculation, you can't get pregnant.

- You can't get pregnant if you have sex standing up.

- You can't get pregnant if you're on your period.

- You can't get pregnant if you use two condoms.

- You can't get pregnant if the female is on top.

- You can't get pregnant if he pulls it out before he releases.

- You can't get pregnant if you don't have an orgasm.

- You can't get pregnant if you drink Mountain Dew after sex.
- You can only get an STD once.

Parents, you need to discuss each of these myths—and that's what they are, myths, not truths—with your daughters. She needs to be very clear about what is true and what is false.

Lies Men Tell

Your daughter needs to be well prepared for the lies she's going to hear from males. There's nothing a man will not say in order to have sex with your daughter. Listed below are some of the classic male statements.

- If you love me, you'll have sex with me.
- If you loved me, you would not make me wear a condom.
- Act like a woman, not like a girl.
- If you won't give me what I want, someone else will.
- I'll be careful.
- Trust me.

Arm your daughter with the following classic statements. Hopefully they will protect her and keep her strong until she's ready.

- Your looks may attract him, but only your spirit will keep him.
- You don't need a man or a baby to have self-worth.
- God gave you one of His greatest gifts. Keep it, cherish it, protect it, and only give it to your husband.
- I commend the thousands of Black girls who wear chastity rings and have taken an oath of abstinence until marriage. The media ignore abstinent girls, but we applaud them.

Raising Black Girls

In the next chapter, we will look at the safety factors affecting your daughter.

Chapter 14: Safety

I am dedicating this chapter to DeCarol Delony, a beautiful mother who had two sons and one daughter. DeCarol's 17-year-old daughter was dating an 18-year-old male of whom she disapproved. One day in 2014, DeCarol came home from work to find both her daughter and the boyfriend in the house even though he was not supposed to be there. She had told her daughter that she did not want him in her house. The boyfriend did not like the mother either, and he killed DeCarol, put her body in a bag and put the bag in the trunk of a car. She was found dead several days later. Please share this unfortunate tragedy with your daughter. Your daughter's selection of a boyfriend could be a matter of life and death for the entire family.

This chapter is about keeping our daughters safe, and safety begins at home. Forty-six percent of children who are raped are raped by their relatives. Many daughters are afraid to tell their mothers, and those who do tell are often disappointed at their mothers' responses. Many mothers refuse to believe that a rape occurred.

In some homes, there are simply too many uncles, boyfriends, and stepfathers in close proximity to our daughters. Our girls are sleeping in fear in their own homes, so much so that they put knives under their pillows to fight off relatives. They don't tell anyone, like an older brother, out of fear that they could get beat up or killed by the uncles, boyfriends, and stepdaddies.

Our girls deserve better. They deserve a safe home. If there's no other place in the world that our daughters should feel safe, it's at home. Generally, I believe permissive and neglectful parents often carelessly put their children in harm's way. Generally, I don't believe authoritative or authoritarian parents would knowingly risk endangering the lives of their children.

Raising Black Girls

School is another dangerous place for girls. More than 50 percent of Black girls report that they have been involved in at least one fight during their K–12 experience.[45] The rule in school is that if someone is bothering you, you should report it to a professional. The problem is, many girls say they do not receive the protection they need from educators to ward off bullies. As a result, they feel they have no choice but to protect themselves.

Twelve percent of all Black girls are suspended. There are many reasons why girls are involved in fights. They fight over the following:

- Boyfriends
- Girlfriends
- "Good" hair
- Skin complexion
- Gossip
- Being called a name
- Social media
- Jealousy
- Neighborhood turf
- Cafeteria and food
- Gym skirmishes
- Clothing
- Eye contact
- Attitudes
- Whatever

Having a boyfriend has become dangerous for too many Black girls.

- Females report they are sexually harassed by a boyfriend at least once.
- 89 percent of girls report sexual harassment.

- 61 percent report some physical altercation.
- 47 percent report that they have been raped.
- Females between the ages of 16 and 24 experience the highest per capita rates of domestic violence.
- 15 percent of teens have been punched with a closed fist by their boyfriends.
- 27 percent have been slapped, grabbed, or pushed.
- 5 percent have been threatened or attacked with a weapon.
- 30 percent of all teen females who were killed were killed by a current or former boyfriend.
- 23 percent of teens involved in an abusive relationship never reported the abuse.[46]

Girls can be vocal with their friends and parents, but quiet as a mouse with boyfriends. This is a self-esteem issue. There's a distinction between mate-esteem and self-esteem. Black girls must reach the conclusion that they are valuable. Ultimately, they must reach this conclusion for themselves, but you can encourage them, and never give up. They must come to value themselves more than they value a mate.

Males know who they can hit and who they can't. They know which females demand respect and which ones don't. Black girls must stand up to their boyfriends and let them know certain things will not be tolerated. Parents must teach them how to do that.

The Streets

Many of our girls live in dangerous neighborhoods where males have no problem running sexual trains on young girls. In addition:

- In 2013, there were 854 Black female victims of homicide.
- There are 100,000 female members of gangs.

- 35 percent of female gang members are African American. There are more than 35,000 Black females in gangs.
- 60 percent of Black girls have witnessed a shooting.
- Many Black girls are suffering from Post-Traumatic Slavery Disorder.[47]

Unfortunately, many Black female homicide victims were simply walking down the street, sitting on a porch, and even sleeping in their bed, the victims of stray bullets.

Sex Trafficking

This is a $64 billion worldwide industry. In the U.S., 62 percent of sex trafficking victims are African American, 94 percent are female, and 87 percent are under 25 years old.[48]

Did you know that the biggest day for sex trafficking is Super Bowl Sunday?

Drug dealers have found that if they sell drugs, at some point their supply will run out and they will have to buy more. But if they sell women, they never run out. Young female prostitutes work 18 to 20 hours per day. Pimps are making around $300,000 per year by selling the bodies of Black teenage females.

Sex trafficking and runaway youth are parallel problems.

- 800,000 children go missing annually.
- 47 percent of runaway youth report conflict with a parent/guardian in the home.
- More than 50 percent of youth in shelters or on the streets report that their parents told them to leave or knew they were leaving but did not care.
- 80 percent of homeless and runaway girls report having been sexually or physically abused.
- 34 percent of runaway youth report sexual abuse before leaving home.

Chapter 14: Safety

- More than 70 percent of runaway youth are considered to be in danger.
- 7 percent of youth and runaways in homeless youth shelters and 14 percent of youth on the street have traded sex for money, food, shelter, and drugs.
- 32 percent of runaway and homeless youth have attempted suicide at some point in their lives.[49]

Are Black girls safer walking down the street today in an urban environment, or were they safer in Mississippi in 1815? In 1815, if a Black girl was walking through the fields, the person she would feel safest walking toward her would be a Black woman, a Black man second, and a White woman third. The person she would feel the least comfortable walking toward her late at night in the fields of Mississippi would be a White man.

Two hundred years later it's midnight, and she's walking through the streets of an urban area. Many women have told me that the first person she would want to see walking toward her would still be a Black woman, a White woman second, a White male third, and the last person she would want to see late at night walking toward her would be a Black man.

A Black man took advantage of her in her house.

A Black man took advantage of her while on a date.

Her pimp took advantage of her on the streets.

Until the Black community addresses the deeper issues of Post-Traumatic Slavery Disorder, incarceration of Black males, and high levels of unemployment, Black women and girls need to be taught to defend themselves. Therefore, I'm recommending that parents and caregivers enroll their daughters in self-defense classes and martial arts. Take them to the gun range and teach them the proper way to use a gun. Our girls must exercise more.

Raising Black Girls

We must protect our girls. Our girls deserve better.

In the last chapter, we will address some very important issues, not previously discussed.

Chapter 15: Some Closing Afterthoughts

There are so many areas to cover when discussing how best to raise girls. In this final chapter, we will explore issues that were not covered in depth previously, but that are still very important.

Other Relatives and Foster Care

We devoted chapters to mothers and fathers, but other relatives also deserve our attention. Not all Black children are reared solely by a mother and/or father. Seventeen percent of our children live with a grandparent and one or both of the biological parents. Unfortunately, large numbers of children are reared without either parent. When this occurs, 64 percent of the time the grandparents raise the children.[50]

Twenty-six percent of all children in foster care are African American, totaling 104,000 children. The following list describes the types of living situations and institutions that care for them.

- 47 percent are in non-relative foster care.
- 28 percent are in relative foster family homes.
- 9 percent are in institutions.
- 6 percent are in group homes.
- 6 percent are on trial home visits.
- 4 percent are in pre-adoptive homes.
- 1 percent run away.
- 1 percent are in supervised independent living facilities.[51]

I want to empower grandparents, aunts, uncles, cousins, foster parents, and institutional providers. There are five things I'd like you to consider as you're raising a female child:

1. What is your parenting style? Is it permissive, neglectful, authoritarian, or authoritative?
2. Take the parenting quiz that appears in Chapter 4.
3. Review the goals sheet also in Chapter 4. What goals do you have for the child you're raising?

4. What is your ratio of praise to criticism? Do you criticize more than you praise? Is it an equal ratio between praise and criticism? Our children need more praise than criticism.
5. Quality conversation is important. What kinds of things do you talk about? How frequently do you discuss academics and what she will be doing after she graduates from high school? Notice I said "after she graduates." The assumption is that she is not going to drop out of school.

Health and Nutrition

I want to dedicate this section to 13-year-old Mo'ne Davis, the brilliant pitcher from Philadelphia, and Ida Keeling who set the 100-meter record for 99-year-olds in 2014.

Chapter 15: Some Closing Afterthoughts

Have you taught your daughter about the importance of diet, exercise, health, and nutrition? No group is more overweight than Black females at 42 percent. Consider the following:

- How much water does your daughter drink per day? Does she drink more water than any other drink?
- How much fruit does she consume daily?
- How many raw vegetables does she consume daily?
- Does she consume more raw food or cooked food?
- Do you monitor her salt and sugar consumption?
- What percent of her diet is fried?
- How many minutes does she exercise daily?
- Can your daughter swim?
- Does she smoke?
- Does she consume alcohol?
- Does she use illegal drugs?
- Have you taught your daughter how to avoid being overweight?
- Have you taught your daughter how to avoid fibroid tumors?
- Have you taught your daughter how to avoid high blood pressure?
- Have you taught your daughter how to avoid diabetes?
- Have you taught your daughter how to avoid arthritis and rheumatism?
- Have you taught your daughter how to avoid heart disease?
- Have you taught your daughter how to avoid cancer?

Divorce

We mentioned earlier that only 28 percent of Black children live with their fathers. This does not mean that both biological parents are present. Most parents have no idea of the impact divorce has on children. They may not be as resilient as you think. They may not say much, but there could be rage boiling inside. What has been the impact of divorce or lack of marriage on our daughters? When parents divorce, daughters may experience some of these responses:

- Anger
- Depression
- Hopelessness
- Distrust
- Hair loss
- Silence
- Anxiety
- Withdrawn
- Promiscuous
- Declining grades
- Suspensions
- Confusion over two sets of house rules.

Most divorced parents believe their children are fine. In 90 percent of divorce cases, the children are suffering in silence.[52]

History and Culture

Have you taught your daughter how to love her history and culture?

- Does she know more history before 1620 or after 1620?
- Is your daughter proud to be Black?
- How does she feel about the continent of Africa?
- Have you taught her to recognize and resist racism, sexism, classism, colorism, and Post-Traumatic Slavery Disorder?
- Does your daughter know the name of the first Black female doctor?
- Does your daughter know the Nguzo Saba?
- Does your daughter know the Seven Cardinal Virtues of Ma'at?
- Does your daughter know the names of African queens?

Listed below are the names of some of the more well-known African queens. Have your daughters research, write about, critique, and appreciate these powerful women.

Chapter 15: Some Closing Afterthoughts

- Queen Hatshepsut – Egypt
- Queen Nefertiti – Egypt
- Queen Candace – Ethiopia
- Queen Nandi – Zulus of Southern Africa
- Queen Yaa Asantewaa – Ashanti Empire (modern day Ghana)
- Queen Nefertari – Egypt
- Queen Nzingah – Ndongo and Matamba Kingdoms (modern day Angola)
- Queen Makeda – Ethiopia
- Queen Tiye – Egypt
- Queen Cleopatra (Yes! Queen Cleopatra was Black!) – *Egypt*

Can your daughter name 20 famous Black women outside of sports and entertainment?

- Harriet Tubman
- Ida B. Wells
- Rosa Parks
- Mary Church Terrell
- Mary Cary
- Crystal Fauset
- Mary Pleasant
- Winnie Mandela
- Barbara Sizemore
- Mary McLeod Bethune
- Ella Baker
- Madame C. J. Walker
- Sojourner Truth
- Dorothy Height
- Fannie Lou Hamer
- Mary Bowser
- Bessie Coleman
- Frances Harper
- Maggie Walker
- Septima Clark
- Shirley Chisholm
- Angela Davis
- Oprah Winfrey
- Jocelyn Elders

Raising Black Girls

- Carol Moseley Braun
- Marian Wright Edelman
- Michelle Obama
- Jo Ann Robinson
- Elaine Brown
- Condoleezza Rice
- Coretta Scott King
- Oseola McCarty
- Ellen Johnson Sirleaf (President of Liberia)
- Joyce Banda (President of Malawi)

- Maxine Waters
- Queen Mother Moore
- Barbara Jordan
- Assata Shakur
- Kathleen Cleaver
- Betty Shabazz
- Maria Stewart
- Catherine Samba-Panza (President of the Central African Republic)

Can your daughter name 10 Black female writers?

- Sojourner Truth
- Nikki Giovanni
- Alice Walker
- Sharon Draper
- Toni Cade Bambara
- Gwendolyn Brooks
- Nannie Helen Burroughs

- Maya Angelou
- Sonia Sanchez
- Terry McMillan
- Toni Morrison
- Zora Neale Hurston
- Lorraine Hansberry
- bell hooks

Chapter 15: Some Closing Afterthoughts

- Isabel Wilkerson
- Margaret Walker
- Pearl Cleage
- Paule Marshall
- J. California Cooper
- Sister Souljah
- Ntozake Shange
- Ida B. Wells
- Donna Marie Williams
- Venus Evans-Winters
- Jamaica Kincaid
- Iyanla Vanzant
- Monique Morris
- Paula Giddings
- Patricia Hills Collins
- Octavia Butler
- Audre Lorde
- Rita Dove
- Kimberla Roby
- Beverly Sheftall
- Phillis Wheatley
- Harriet Jacobs
- Mary Lewis
- Dierdre Paul
- Joyce Ladner
- Melissa Harris-Perry
- Ruth Brown

Money Management and Economic Development

Let me begin with a beautiful story about Taylor Moxey. While most little girls are busy playing with their dolls or other kid stuff, eight-year-old Taylor Moxey is well on her way to what she dreams of doing in later life: opening her own bakery. Taylor, who bakes her own cakes and packs them into individual boxes, already has quite a few regular customers around her Miami, Florida home, including CitiBank. Taylor's business climbed rapidly after she won the KISS Country Midtown Miami Cornbread Competition in 2014, in which she beat trained adult chefs to take home first prize.

Raising Black Girls

I felt it was important to tell Taylor's story because the average single Black female has a net worth of $5.00.[53] When you compare that to the net worth of Whites at $101,000, it is obvious that we need to do a better job of preparing Black females to understand money management and economic development. This does not start on their 21st birthday. This education needs to start early, when you give them their first allowance. Ten percent of their allowance should go to God as a tithe, and another 10 percent should be saved. We need to teach Black girls the importance of tithing and saving.

We need to teach our girls how to operate a checking account. They must learn the importance of a credit score. We need to teach our daughters how to develop a budget. Show your daughter the budget for your household so that she has a greater appreciation for money management and the financial impact of her actions in the home. For example, when she turns on the lights, the electric bill increases. When she turns up the thermostat, the heating bill increases. Children need to learn early about the expenses that are involved with running a household.

We need to teach our daughters entrepreneurship. Work with your daughter to develop a business plan. Honestly ask yourself if telling your daughter that she should get a good education to get a good job is the best advice to give her. Or would it be wiser to tell her to get a good education in order to start her own business?

Let's teach our girls about the stock market. Open up a mutual fund for your daughter. You can open a mutual fund for as little as $50. That's what my father did for me. Every year on my birthday, he'd add more to the mutual fund. Periodically, review the stock market and its movement with your daughter. I'd recommend the Vanguard Total Stock Market Fund. It provides the greatest amount of diversity and the lowest operating cost.

Teach your daughter about real estate and how people in the neighborhood are acquiring properties in foreclosure and tax lien certificates. They are rehabbing those properties and selling them or renting them out to tenants. While many African Americans think the best way to acquire wealth is either in sports, entertainment, or selling drugs, other people are acquiring their wealth in entrepreneurship, the stock market, and real estate.

I encourage you to watch *Shark Tank* with your daughter. Expose her to *Black Enterprise* and their Teenpreneur Conferences for ages 19 and under. Give your child the manual *Entrepreneurship: Owning Your Future* from The National Foundation for Teaching Entrepreneurship.[54]

Last, but not least, teach your daughter the importance of trying to live debt free, to live within her means. Please provide your daughter with articles, magazines, and books about economics and money management. There are thousands of Black females, including girls, who are starting businesses and doing very well. Expose your daughter to her peers who are becoming millionaires before their 18th birthday.

Household Responsibilities
- Does your daughter do chores?
- Does she know how to clean a house?

- Does she know how to wash clothes, specifically white, colored, and dark clothes?
- Does she know how to iron?
- Does she know how to sew?
- Does she know how to cook a full meal?
- Does she know how to bake?
- Does she know how to decorate and design a house?
- Does she know how to operate the circuit breaker?
- Does she know how to replace furnace filters?
- Does she know the importance of running hot water down the drains?
- Regarding auto maintenance, does she know the importance of changing the oil, checking the battery, checking the air pressure on tires, and rotating the tires? Can your daughter change a flat tire?
- Does she understand that every machine in the house requires some degree of maintenance?

Corporal Punishment

- I had decided not to write about spanking because those who believe in spanking will continue and those who don't will continue to condemn those who do. I read an article in writing this book that changed my mind. A mother was called to the school because her daughter was missing tutorial classes. When they both left the school, the daughter was defiant and felt her mother was being too strict about her attending the classes to improve her failing grades. The mother slapped her in the face in the parking lot.
- I am an advocate of spanking, but this was not spanking. I believe spanking should be on the buttocks and no bruises. I also believe the parent should be in complete emotional control. I also do not believe spanking should be the only form of discipline. I believe the order should be praise of good behavior, clearly explain the rules and consequences,

warning, denial, exclusion or isolation and then spanking. I remember when my children, were younger, I would tell them to get my belt, go to their room and wait for me. When I would arrive hours later they had already spanked themselves emotionally.

- Let me return back to the mother and daughter in the parking lot. The daughter after being slapped ran back into the school and reported the abuse to the school. The mother was arrested and the daughter was placed in Child Protective Services. If the daughter thought she had been abused there is a much greater chance she will encounter abuse in this setting. It is also unfortunate that the mother is now in jail and it all started over missing tutoring classes to correct failing grades. I could write another book on the above, but I defer to you and your daughter discussing the above.

After High School

What are your daughter's plans after high school? Does she plan to go to college? Will it be a junior college, business college, online college, or a four-year university? Will she attend a school in the city, out of town, out of state, or even out of the country? Have you budgeted for tuition, room and board, and other living expenses?

The time to prepare to send your daughter to college is at birth and not her senior year. If you save $200 month for 10 years and invest at 6.8 percent return you will have $34,400. If you borrow $34,400, you will pay $390 per month. Too many parents are borrowing rather than saving for college.

What are your daughter's goals for her future? What will be her college major? Can she give a different career for each letter of the alphabet?

Has your daughter considered developing a blue-collar skill? Remember:

- Child care workers are paid $8.00 per hour.
- Secretaries are paid $10 to $15.00 per hour.
- Bus and truck drivers are paid $20 to $40.00 per hour.
- Construction workers are paid $25 to $50.00 per hour.
- Plumbers, electricians, and carpenters are paid $50 to $75.00 per hour.

Has your daughter considered the military? While African Americans are 14 percent of the population, Black females represent 31 percent of all females in the military.

Does your daughter have a strong work ethic? How long can your daughter stay in your house? How long can she stay in your house without working? How long can your daughter stay in your house without going to college?

Crime and Incarceration

Unfortunately, some of our girls are not going to college, workforce, or the military. They are becoming incarcerated at an alarming rate. The stats are quite disturbing. Many of our girls are in crisis.

- 35,000 African American females are members of gangs.
- 25 percent of African American females, at one time or another, will be involved in shoplifting.
- Many Black females are incarcerated because they were holding or transporting their boyfriend's drugs or guns.
- 1 of every 19 Black girls will be involved in the penal system.
- Sterilization is now taking place illegally in some prisons.
- Many Black mothers have become separated from or lost their children because of incarceration. [55]

A Love for Jesus

In my opinion, I've saved the best for last. Does your daughter have a love for Jesus? Does she know Him? Do you know Him?

Chapter 15: Some Closing Afterthoughts

Have you testified about how good God has been to you? Does your daughter have a relationship with Him? Does she talk to Him? Does she listen to Him? Does she pray to Him? Has she seen *you* pray to Him? Has she experienced *your* relationship with Him?

Does your daughter know His Word? How frequently does your daughter read the Bible? Do you have Bible study with her?

Is church attendance optional in your house?

Does your daughter love Him enough to pray publicly in front of her friends to Him? Do they know your daughter is saved and has a relationship with Jesus?

There's no greater gift you could give your daughter than to introduce her to Him. When you celebrate Christmas make sure your daughter understands He is the reason for the season!

Notes

1. U. S. Statistical Abstract 2012, last revised July 17, 2013. www.census.gov/prod/www/statistical_abstract.html;

Michael Holzman, *Minority Students and Public Education* (Briarcliff Manor: Chelmsford Press, 2013); Trip Gabriel, "Proficiency of Black Students Is Found to Be Far Lower Than Expected," *New York Times,* November 9, 2010. http://www.nytimes.com/2010/11/09/education/09gap.html?_r=0; Catherine Gewertz, "NAEP [National Assessment of Educational Progress] Scores Inch Up in Math, Reading," *Education Week,* November 13, 2013. http://www.edweek.org/ew/articles/2013/11/13/12naep-2.h33.html;

Monique Morris, *Black Stats* (New York: New Press, 2014), 16; Jane David, "What Research Says about Grade Retention," *Educational Leadership,* March 2008, 83-84. http://www.ascd.org/publications/educational-leadership/mar08/vol65/num06/Grade-Retention.aspx; Council of the Great City Schools, Washington, DC. http://www.cgcs.org; Caralee Adams, "Most Students Aren't Ready for College, ACT Data Show," *Hechinger Report,* August 21, 2013. http://www.hechinger report.org/content/

Notes

most-students-arent-ready-for-college-act-data-show 12951/; *The Urgency of Now: The Schott 50 State Report on Public Education and Black Males* (Cambridge, MA: The Schott Foundation, 2012). http://blackboysreport.org; Marcia Greenberger, et al., *When Girls Don't Graduate, We All Fail* (Washington, DC: National Women's Law Center, 2007). when_girls_dont_ graduate.pdf; F. C. Frazier, et al., *Placing Black Girls at Promise: Report of the Rise Sister Rise Study, Executive Summary* (Columbus, OH: Ohio Department of Mental Health, 2011). rsr_columbus_executive_summary.pdf; The National Campaign to Prevent Teen and Unplanned Pregnancy, *Under Pressure: What African-American Teens Aren't Telling You about Sex, Love, and Relationships* (Washington, DC: The National Campaign, 2011). https://thenationalcampaign.org/resource/under-pressure; Linda Eastman, *Raising African American Girls* (Prospect, KY: Professional Woman Publishing, 2009), 123-124. Juleyka Lantigua-Williams, "Missing and Black—Special Report," *JET* Magazine, April 8, 2013. http://www.jetmag.com/insidejet/cover-story-fade-to-black/; Jesse Muhammad, "Calls from Runaway, Throwaway Youth Skyrocket, *Final Call,* June 9, 2010. http://jessemuhammad.blogs.

141

finalcall.com/2010/06/calls-from-runaway-throwaway-youth.html; National Runaway Switchboard, "Why They Run: An In-Depth Look at America's Runaway Youth," The National Runaway Safeline, May 2010. http://www.1800runaway.org/learn/rescarch/why_they_run/report; National Safe Place, Youth Runaway Prevention. http://nationalsafeplace.org; www.blacknews.com/news/congressman-robin-kelly; www.blackgenocide.org

2. *U. S. Statistical Abstract 2013.*

3. "Watch Kevin Durant's Powerful, Emotional MVP Acceptance Speech," *USA Today*, May 6, 2014. http://ftw.usatoday.com/2014/05/kevin-durant-mvp-speech-mom

4. Michael Clark, "Mother and Adoptive Daughter Found on Doorstep Celebrate 18 Years," The Grio, July 11, 2014. http://thegrio.com/2014.07/11/mother-and-adoptive-daughter-found-on-doorstep-celebrate-18-years

Notes

5. David Chang, "Delaware Mom after 4-Year-Old Gives Heroin to Kids at Daycare: Police," NBC, October 7, 2014. http://www.nbcphiladelphia.com/news/local/Arrested-After-4-Year-Old-Gives-Heroin-to-Kids-at-Daycare-Police-278315441.html

6. *U. S. Statistical Abstract 2013.*

7. *U. S. Statistical Abstract 2013*2 reports there are 4 million single parents and 90 percent are female; therefore there are 400,000 single parent fathers.

8. Tara Culp-Ressler, "The Myth of the Absent Black Father," Think Progress, January 16, 2014. www.thinkprogress.org/health/myth-absent-black-fathers

9. David Finkelhor, Heather Hammer, and Andrea Sedlak, "Sexually Assaulted Children: National Estimates and Characteristics," National Incidence Studies of Missing, Abducted, Runaway, and Throwaway Children. Washington, DC: National Criminal Justice Reference Service, 2014. https://www.ncjrs.org/.../214383.pdf

10. Denene Millner, "The Attack against Black Girl Beauty," May 20, 2011. www.mybrownbaby.com/2011/05/the-attack-against-black-girl-beauty

11. "Lupita Nyong'o Delivers Moving 'Black Women in Hollywood' Acceptance Speech," *Essence,* February 28, 2014. www.essence.com/lupita-nyongo-delivers-moving-black-women-in-hollywood

12. "A Beautiful Dark-Skinned Woman Explains How Her Mother Made Her Bullet-Proof against Colorism," Naturally Moi, April 14, 2014. www.naturallymoi.com/2014/07/a-beautiful-dark-skinned-woman-explains-how-her-mother-made-her-bullet-proof-against-colorism

13. "I'm Insecure Because I'm Black," Is It Normal? http://isitnormal.com/story-im-insecure-because-im-black

14. "Patti LaBelle Regrets Cosmetic Surgery," *Toronto Sun*, May 23, 2014. http://www.torontosun.com/2014/05/23/patti-labelle-regrets-cosmetic-surgery

15. Nomalanga Mhlauli-Moses, "Whoopi Goldberg's Mom Told Her to Work Hard as She Was Not 'the Prettiest,'" www.successfulblackwoman.com/?p=2444

16. Sylvia Obell, "Viola Davis Addresses Being Called 'Less Classically Beautiful' by NY Times Critic," *Essence*, September 26, 2014. www.essence.com/2014/09/26/viola-davis-addresses-being-called-less-classically-beautiful-ny-times/

17. Legal Defense Fund, "Brown at 60: The Doll Test," NACCP. www.naacpldf.org/brown-at-60-the-doll-test

18. "Study: White and Black Children Biased toward Lighter Skin," CNN, May 13, 2010. http://www.cnn.com/2010/US/05/13/doll.study/

19. Hamilton Nolan, "Straight Outta Compton Casting Call Is Racist as Hell," Gawker, July 17, 2014. http://gawker.com/straight-outta-compton-casting-call-is-racist-as-hell-1606524197

20. "Study Shows $235K Pay Gap between Attractive and Unattractive People," July 23, 2014. www.naturallymoi.com/study-shows-235k-pay-gap-between-attractive-and-unattractive-people

21. The Association of Black Psychologists, "On Dark Girls," June 23, 2013. www.abpsi.org/pdf/Dark_Girls_ABPsi_ARTICLE_JUNE_23_2013_Dr%20Grills.pdf

22. Ibid.

23. "Natural Hair Now," *Ebony,* January 2014, 137; www.blacklikemoi.com/2013/07/more-african-american-women-are-going-natural

24. Rachel Loussaint, "Why So Soon? A Girl's First Perm," Madame Noire, March 19, 2012. http://madamenoire.com/147226/why-so-soon-a-girls-first-perm/

25. Beth Galvin, "STUDY: Hair Relaxers Raise Black Women's Risk of Fibroids," My Fox Atlanta, January 21, 2014. www.myfoxatlanta.com/study/hair-relaxers-raise-black-womens-risk-of-fibroids

26. Fiona Macrae, "Hair Dyes Used by Millions of Women Are Linked to Chemicals That Can Cause Cancer," *Daily Mail*, February 19, 2013. http://www.dailymail.co.uk/article-2281413/Hair-dye-used-millions-women-linked-chemicals-cause-cancer.html

27. Joseph Nordqvist, "African American Women Avoid Exercise Because of Hair Maintenance," *Medical News Today*, December 19. 2012. http://www.medicalnewstoday.com/articles/254281.php

28. Op. cit., *Minority Students and Public Education, Black Stats, U. S. Statistical Abstract 2012.*

29. Anthony Johnson, "NYC Department of Education Investigating Death of Omotayo Adeoye, Who Was Accused of Cheating," WABC-TV New York, June 7, 2014. http://7online.com/education-doe-investigating-death-of-student-caught-cheating-on-test/87379

30. Tina Rosenberg, "The Power of Talking to Your Baby," *NY Times,* April 10, 2013. http://opinionator.blogs.nytimes.com/2013/04/10/the-power-of-talking-to-your-baby/?_r=0; Amanda Askwith, "The Importance of Parent Involvement," http://www.slideshare.net/AskwithAmanda/the-importance-of-parent-nvolvement?related=2

31. Victoria Rideout, Ulla Foehr, and Donald Roberts, *Generation M²: Media in the Lives of 8- to 18-Year-Olds.* Menlo Park, CA: Kaiser Family Foundation (January 2010). http://kaiserfamilyfoundation.files.wordpress.com/2013/04/8010.pdf

32. Ibid.

33. Ibid.

34. Ibid.

35. Ibid.

36. Ibid.

37. Ibid.

38. Ibid.

39. Dr. Venus Evans-Winters. *Black Girls Media Declaration.* http://www.blackgirlsmediapledge.com

40. Jonel Aleccia, "Obesity Linked to Early Puberty in Girls, Study Finds," NBC News, November 3, 2013. http://nbcnews.com/health/kids-health/obesity-linked-early-puberty-girls-study-finds-f8C11514727; P. B. Kaplowitz, et al., "Earlier Onset of Puberty in Girls: Relation to Increased Body Mass Index and Race," *Pediatrics,* August 2001, 108(2): 347-53.

41. Op. cit., *Under Pressure.*

42. Ibid.

43. Ibid.

44. Ibid.

45. Ibid.

46. Ibid.

47. Op. cit., *Raising African American Girls.*

48. United Nations Office on Drugs and Crime. *A Global Report on Trafficking in Persons* Vienna, Austria: Global Report on Trafficking in Persons Unit (2012). https://www.unodc.org/documents-and-analysis/glotip/Trafficking_in_Persons_2012_web.pdf

49. Op. cit., "Missing and Black," *Final Call,* National Runaway Switchboard, National Safe Place.

50. *U. S. Statistical Abstract 2013;* Ann Brenoff, "Pew Study: One in 10 Grandchildren Lives with Grandparents," Huffington Post, September 4, 2013. http://www.huffingtonpost.com/2013/09/04/grandparents-raising-grandchildren_n_3866302.html; Gretchen Livingston, *At Grandmother's House We Stay* (September 4, 2013). Pew Research Center: Social & Demographic Trends. Grandparents_report_final_2013.pdf

51. Child Welfare Information Gateway, *Foster Care Statistics 2012* (2013). U. S. Department of Health and Human Services, Administration for Children & Families. https://www.childwelfare.gov/pubs/factsheets/foster.cfm

52. Khadija Allen, "How Is Divorce Affecting Black Children?" Madame Noire, December 28, 2010. http://madamenoire.com/31853/how-is-divorce-affecting-black-

children-2; Charreah K. Jackson, "9 Interesting Facts About Divorce for Black Couples," *Essence,* July 4, 2013. http://www.essence.com/2013/07/04/9-interesting-facts-about-divorce-black-couples

53. "Study Shows Median Net Worth of Black Women Is Just $5," Financial Juneteenth, May 6, 2014. www.financial juneteenth.com/study-shows-median-net-worth-of-black-women

54. http://www.blackenterprise.com/tag/teenpreneur/; National Foundation for Teaching Entrepreneurship, *Entrepreneurship: Owning Your Future.* New York: Network for Teaching Entrepreneurship. https://www.nfte.com/resources

55. Op. cit., *Black Stats*; "Incarcerated Women," The Sentencing Project. http://www.sentencingproject.org/.../cc_incarcerated_women

153